Colaba

Praise for *Colaba*

'This is the perfect companion for a walk down the Colaba Causeway: a guide who is an insider, who combines the best storytelling instinct of the novelist with the insouciance of the journalist and the persistence of the local historian. Shabnam Minwalla brings us the rapscallions and the ballerinas, the exotic dancers and the poets, the nuns and the murderers in a wonderful guide to the southernmost tip of *urbs prima in Indis*.'—Jerry Pinto

'Colaba comes alive...vividly and delicately. For "Colabawalas" (almost) like myself, it was a deep dive into another era...recreated with love and longing by a gifted writer.'—Shobhaa Dé

'Shabnam is the curious fly on the wall watching the pageant of fame and infamy, elegance and seediness, Colaba's heart and underbelly alike.'—Bachi Karkaria

'Colaba is Bombay's most fabled neighbourhood—and Shabnam Minwalla knows all its stories. She stirs together three generations of family memory of living in the area with fascinating archival research and old-fashioned journalistic groundwork to distil a set of lessons for life that Colaba taught her. There's plenty for readers to learn too—in the most engaging way. *Colaba* helps us see some of the city's most familiar streets and buildings with new eyes.'—Naresh Fernandes

Colaba

The Diamond at the Tip of Mumbai

SHABNAM MINWALLA

SPEAKING TIGER

SPEAKING TIGER BOOKS LLP
125 A, Shahpur Jat, Near Asiad Village
New Delhi - 110049, India

Published by Speaking Tiger Books in hardback 2020

ISBN: 978-93-89958-90-4
eISBN: 978-93-89958-91-1

10 9 8 7 6 5 4 3 2

Typeset in Cardo by SÜRYA, New Delhi
Printed at Chaman Enterprises, New Delhi

For my grandmother, Meryam

Contents

Contents

Saurab Rao

A typical Colaba street.

Preface

If we were to divide neighbourhoods into the haves and the have-nots, Colaba would sit squarely in the second group.

This narrow strip of land—an arthritic index finger crooked in a grey sea—is neither known for its pulchritude nor its places of historical significance. Here are no forts with medieval pasts, tales of tragic queens or echoes of bloody battles. No tallest buildings or longest bridges. Not even a liberal sprinkling of Bollywood stars or shimmering socialites.

Stare out of the tinted window from one of those Bombay Safari buses, and you will see monsoon-battered buildings, flapping cotton skirts, sparkly-shoe stalls, Blue Heaven Beauty Parlour, Lucky Collection, Ohmazing Fast Food, fruit carts, Teenage, Hampton Court, Sunita, Connaught Mansion, Doggy Articles—which makes it even more difficult to crack the mystery of Colaba's quirky charm and cosy-but-cool reputation.

What Colaba doesn't have is easy to list. What Colaba does have is not. Its qualities are concealed by the voluminous skirts and peeling paint. As is the precise alchemy that transforms this muddle of crumbling buildings and double-parked cars into a land of extraordinary characters and ideas; that allows this paltry protrusion of rocks and cement to occupy such a wide expanse of the imagination.

Of course, Colaba has something that the rest of Bombay lacks—a clutch of must-see landmarks and Tripadvisor-worthy attractions. So, no matter whether they land at Chhatrapati Shivaji Maharaj International Airport or hop off a train at Chhatrapati Shivaji Maharaj Terminus, visitors to the city are likely to make their way southwards. After all, they can hardly come to Mumbai and ignore the Gateway of India. And if they're braving the traffic anyway, they might as well wander beneath the opalescent dome of the museum, (Chhatrapati Shivaji Maharaj Vastu Sangrahalaya) and stroll past its jewel-bright miniatures and stuffed flamingoes, frozen in the middle of ballet routines. After which they usually follow the advice of the guidebooks and drop in at Leopold Café for a plate of salt-and-pepper prawns and a gawp at the bullet-riddled façade of this venerable eatery.

These postcard personalities are, however, only a small part of Colaba's appeal. Much greater is the role played by a cast of intangibles. There are the warm, fuzzy feelings that are tough to name. And the abstract nouns that are tricky to spell (words like cosmopolitanism, tolerance and multiculturalism that we meet all the time but that suddenly acquire heft and meaning in this corner of the city). And the slow realization that this old-fashioned neighbourhood—a babel of tongues, a potpourri of aromas and stinks—is central to the soul of Mumbai.

This was something we grasped on that acrid, blood-splattered night of November 2008, when flames licked the indigo sky and bullets zigzagged Colaba Causeway (some of which are still lodged in the walls of Leopold Café). Newspapers around the world declared that terrorists had struck at the 'heart of Mumbai'. For once, they didn't exaggerate.

Subsequent reports made it clear that the killers wanted to destroy more than lives and landmarks, they wanted to shatter the spirit of the city. That they had sought the symbolic heart of Mumbai with surgical precision—and homed in on Colaba.

It's ironic, then, that Colaba has moved further and further away from the geographical centre of Mumbai. As the city leaps across creeks and bridges, gobbling mangroves, saltpans and fishing villages and throwing up clusters of towers and malls, it sometimes feels as if Colaba has come a full circle. That it has returned to what it was for so many centuries—an inconvenient outpost. The only difference is that the malodorous creek has been replaced by traffic-choked streets. And the snakes and jackals by predators of a different kind.

Even if the Colaba pin codes have lost their cachet, the whimsy and magic linger. A couple of years ago, I found myself sharing a taxi in Srinagar with an actor-turned-economist who described his not-entirely-happy years in Mumbai. 'What would you know, anyway,' he snorted. 'You live in the best corner of India. Colaba is…Colaba.'

I'm not sure if Colaba is the best corner of India. I'm not sure it even matters. What is incontrovertible is that Colaba is Colaba—a distinct dot on the map of India, with a distinct story that must be told.

1. Home

'What is unique and, especially charming, is the fact that it is a truly cosmopolitan neighbourhood. There is a high concentration of Parsis, Sindhis and Dawoodi Bohras, but there are people from all other communities as well. And, most importantly, everyone has always felt welcome. Unlike other areas in Mumbai that have a dominant religious affiliation, Colaba has everything—thriving temples, churches of many denominations, multiple mosques, a gurdwara, a Parsi fire temple.

'Colaba is a woman of many parts. There is the vibrant one who gives the come hither look to tourists on the Causeway. The demure one who likes to quietly eat her chicken pattice at Sunshine Snack Bar near Colaba Post Office. And the tough one, who haggles expertly with her customers as she shells prawns on the seafront at Sassoon Dock.

'Although a large number of residents are wealthy and well-connected, there's also a healthy number of people from the middle- and lower-income groups. And although many may

think of people living in Colaba as being "South Bombay snobs" (God knows I've been labelled that enough times!), the fact is that most people here are not classist. Perhaps it comes from the fact that most are at least second or third generation residents and are comfortable in their identity. Colaba has always had a great sense of community.'

—Priya Pathiyan is a senior journalist and passionate Mumbai city tour guide. She lived in the southernmost part of civilian Colaba for thirty years. Her apartment building overlooked the green treetops of the 'military area' as the locals call the Colaba Defence Station.

I WAS 8,688 MILES FROM HOME WHEN REALIZATION CAME. Not with the crash-bang of a thunderclap. But with the imperceptible whisper of a breeze on a clammy Colaba afternoon. It was a murmur that was easy enough to ignore. And ignore it I did.

There were too many things to think about just then. I had wandered as far from Bombay as was possible—at least without the aid of a spacesuit and oxygen mask. I was still adjusting to the blinding sunshine and designer smiles in California. Preoccupied with assignments that needed completing, meals that needed cooking, cereal brands that needed discovering. And, of course, the endless questions that needed answering.

Whenever an American asked where I was from, I replied that I was from India. Then got ready to chat about spicy food and the Taj Mahal. Whenever an Indian—there were enough of us on that university campus to pack a Mumbai local or two—asked the same question, I said that I was from Bombay. Then steeled myself to defend my beloved, maddening city.

Whenever other Bombayites asked the inevitable question, I explained that I was from Colaba. Which was the truest answer of all, even though I didn't know it then. I still thought of Colaba as a mere address. A fuddy-duddy one at that. The southernmost tip of a city that was sprinting northwards. A collection of leaf-fringed streets and tired buildings; desultory shops with names like 'Sapna-Suhana: The Worst' and 'Dit: Rendezvous D'Art'. An area of dead Englishmen rather than living Bollywood stars.

Not exactly what your average teenager wanted out of life, the universe and everything. On the other hand, Los Angeles—at least in theory—was exactly what the average twenty-something desired. It was a city of blond waiters and shop assistants in tight, black clothes, edgy glamour and diamond-scattered waters.

Why then was I dreaming of the fishy tip of ramshackle Bombay, surrounded by a flat, soupy sea? Of red BEST buses lumbering out of Colaba bus station? Of mornings spent in a cobwebbed building stairwell in Old Cuffe Parade, waiting for Voli Mohammed Halterers to halter/alter a hulking pair of jeans into a skinny Size 0?

Why did I now see what I'd barely registered before? The extraordinary energy on those haphazard streets.

The casual acceptance of differences and similarities. That indefinable something that is the stuff of Beatles songs and courtly sonnets. That democratic racket of church bells, Ganpati visarjans, Moharram processions and *The Best of ABBA*; spiced with an indignant 'Konna baap ni Diwali' as you approach the gate of Cusrow Baug; and topped with 'bunjoos' when you traverse the tourist strip of Colaba Causeway, where pavement stalls proudly announce that they 'spik French, Spanis, Rusun'.

Perhaps distance was playing a double game. On the one hand it offered perspective. On the other, it daubed reality with the gloss of nostalgia—concealing cracks and painting a bright canvas of people, languages, views; making it impossible to reconcile with the darkness overtaking the city during the deadly December of 1992 and January of 1993.

As riots ripped through Dharavi and Dongri, the Bombay of my memories was revealed as a flimsy illusion. The real Bombay was a cut-paste of Pydhonie and Parel; Mazagaon and Bhuleshwar—neighbourhoods where I was familiar with the superficial layer of cement and steel but not with the anger and fear that slithered underneath.

There was only one patch of my city that I knew up, down and sideways. The spindly promontory that extended from Prong's Reef to Prince of Wales Museum (now renamed Chhatrapati Shivaji Maharaj Vastu Sanghralaya). The area called Colaba. Here, I knew the shortcuts and surreptitious dalliances; the precise strip of Garden Road that turned slippery in the rain; the faint footprints of the past, not yet erased by the hurly-burly of the present.

After all, Colaba was the Tupperware neighbourhood that had contained my girlhood. Its mix-and-match streets had imparted life lessons that no one else had taught:

- Never peep into a crowded church till you know whether the protagonist is upright or supine.
- For every bottle cap, there is a perfect bottle out there somewhere.
- Variety, diversity and eccentricity are the salt, pepper, chilli flakes of life.

As a schoolgirl in a sacky, beige uniform, I spent the greater part of each day on Convent Street, a little lane off Colaba Causeway that boasted two sizeable schools. The two schools shared a common wall, which made it easy for the assorted 'snakes in the grass' and 'disruptive elements' in my strict, all-girls school to drop notes to the boys in the not-so-strict co-ed school next door.

Our school was bursting at the seams with the daughters of Convent-education-seeking parents. As a result, the nuns had rented rooms in the smushy-banana-yellow mansion next door. Schoen House was a crumbling pile, complete with a pillared porch and lingering air of sadness. Our junior school was housed on the ground floor, but the rest of the mansion appeared largely uninhabited—an aberration in our houseful city.

Schoen House had belonged to a Mr Sethna, who had rented it out to various Englishmen and then to a Jewish dentist who had fled Germany. The British incarcerated the unfortunate dentist in a camp for enemy nationals during World War II. What happened next is a mystery—one of the many that inhabit the bylanes of Colaba.

Saurab Rao

Schoen House, which features on the list of haunted houses in Mumbai.

Today the building is veiled in spidery silence; strangulated by roots and court cases; frozen in a time when Colaba was still a place of big skies, open shores and innumerable futures. Walking past the crumbling mansion, it's easy to understand why Schoen House features on the list of haunted houses in Mumbai.

Unfortunately, all that atmosphere and history were

wasted on my six-year-old self and my six-year-old friends. I remember playing Sea, Sand, Water, Land, Mud on the antique steps. But I don't have a single memory of the crocodile gargoyles, arched windows or ornamental moldings of dogs. Or, for that matter, of the residential ghost that is such a favourite with bloggers and tour guides today.

By the time my classmates and I were in Standard 4, we had crossed Convent Street and were back in the main school building: grey and cream; stern and substantial. Sitting in our classrooms, we heard the Angelus at noon and saw the flying buttresses and rose windows of the Wodehouse Cathedral next door. Trailing along high corridors, we glimpsed the white dome of the museum, the red dome of the Taj Mahal hotel, the fanciful cupolas, pediments and turrets of other old-timers.

Truth to tell, few of us were uplifted by the stone flourishes. Or captivated by the histories and shadows that surrounded us. Instead, we were just waiting, waiting, waiting for the school bell to ring at 3.50 p.m. (Well, 3.47 during that hectic year when I was Bell Ringer and succumbed to the pleas and pencil pokes of classmates—'Ring it, ring it quickly. She's about to give us homework. Pleasepleaseplease.') The evening bell was a powerful catalyst. The moment it rang, prim maidens transformed into hoydens, tumbling down the staircase towards freedom and home. Some hurried down Convent Street. I, though, was part of the beige river that chattered and clattered onto Nathalal Parekh Marg and turned left at Wodehouse Cathedral.

The Cathedral was a splendid but unpredictable neighbour. Sometimes it spilt over with bridesmaids and beribboned bouquets—and we stood on tiptoes, trying to glimpse the frothy, lacy bride. On other days the mood was sombre—and we averted our eyes and trotted past, unwilling to encounter corpse or coffin.

I walked towards home beneath a canopy of midnight green mango and banyan trees, past the Archbishop's House and Stephen Hall. The Archbishop's House is, of course, the home of the Archbishop of Mumbai. The nuns of our school were inordinately pleased with their grand neighbour and when Cardinal Valerian Gracias, who served between 1953 and 1978, fell ill, we were instructed to perform one good deed a day. These acts of kindness were meant to fill a Basket of Good Deeds that would help the Cardinal recover. We took our mission seriously. We foisted help on bewildered old ladies and suspicious toddlers. We strode about looking purposeful, filching do-gooding opportunities from each other. We filled at least a dozen imaginary baskets to the brim.

Heaven, however, did not succumb to this cajolery. Cardinal Valerian Gracias passed on in 1978. His successor, Cardinal Simon Pimenta, often paraded across the compound to light lamps and inaugurate exhibitions in our school—reducing the nuns to a fluttery, pink-faced delight.

Stephen Hall, down the road, was the abode of The Poor Sisters of Our Lady. The Poor Sisters were the seamstresses responsible for our beige school uniforms, with their box pleats and bags-of-papaya silhouettes. To this already cruel style, the nuns contributed their peculiar brand of genius, transforming generations of schoolgirls—some rosy-cheeked and roly-poly, others tall and willowy—into an army of sexless gnomes.

Partly because of the seamstresses of Stephen Hall and partly because of the hearses, I never liked Nathalal Parekh Marg. Even on the sunniest summer day, the street seemed dank and saturated with schoolgirl sorrows. So, it's ironic that—thanks to spooky Schoen House and graceful Wodehouse Cathedral—this street is a highlight in the walking tour of south Mumbai. Groups of tourists wander past regularly. From their carefree expressions, it's clear that their fifteen-year-old selves were never stuffed into the bespoke, ankle-length sacks crafted by the Poor Sisters of Our Lady.

The first stretch of my homeward trek ended at Buckley Court—a turreted structure that belonged to a Gothic mystery rather than a Bombay crossroad. This was where Fort Convent girls stood every evening, waiting for Campion School to be done for the day. Ten minutes later, the boys would stampede down Cooperage Road with their yells, muddy shoes and poor jokes. We hailed our siblings with relief, eager to put a distance between ourselves and the louring windows of Buckley Court.

Buckley Court was a dilapidated structure with miniature onion domes, stained glass and an arched porch. It must once have been an exquisite example of Indo-Saracenic architecture. By the 1970s, however, it had metamorphosed into a slightly disreputable guesthouse in which the editor Vinod Mehta spent his early years in Bombay. 'I moved next door in Colaba to a Graham Greene kind of hotel called Buckley Court,' he recalled in his memoir, *Lucknow Boy*, years later. 'An extraordinary assortment of oddballs were semi-permanent residents of the seedy establishment—prostitutes of the classy kind; aspiring Urdu poets; Jews waiting for Israeli visas; an Armenian lady with her son who was plotting a rebellion in Turkey; a khadi-clad South African-Indian claiming membership of the African National Congress who waved unauthenticated letters from Nelson Mandela; and a Bollywood comedian Wasti, fallen on bad times, who drank country liquor and regaled the lodgers with lewd stories about Raj Kapoor and Geeta Bali.'

Just as the Orient-meets-Victorian-Gothic style of architecture fit perfectly in the happy muddle of Colaba, so did the miscellaneous denizens of the guesthouse. And it seems a pity that by the time I arrived at that street corner a decade later, the 'love nest' had either shut down or dwindled to its last occupants. We never could tell whether the shadows at the cracked windows belonged to the living or the undead.

Some years later, a 'luxury skyscraper'—shaped to mimic a ship's prow—emerged from the husk of that mansion. The new Buckley Court features extravagant apartments, bean-shaped balconies and stern chowkidars—certainly not the kind of home a self-respecting ghost would choose. Which makes me wonder whether the disgruntled spectres of Buckley Court glided down Nathalal Parekh Marg on a moonless night, checking out real estate along the way, skirting the Archbishop's House for obvious reasons, and Stephen Hall for even more obvious reasons, till they finally moved into the welcoming environs of Schoen House.

Back in the late '70s and early '80s, however, the beings of Buckley Court were still in residence and hurried us on our way. My brother and I had two options. On adventurous evenings, we used the shortcut—trotting down the lonely Accommodation Lane, scaling the wall into Cusrow Baug, galloping across the quiet colony, then one more wall to climb, a knee to skin, and home.

Many know the cream façade and lofty arched entrance of Cusrow Baug. Those who've stepped into this Parsi colony, designed by the English architect Claude Batley, know its serene lawns, neat lanes and floral curtains. But it's only the reckless few—wall-jumpers, shameless trespassers and their ilk—who know the hidden perils of this seemingly tranquil corner of Colaba. For behind the twitching curtains of Cusrow Baug lurk fierce old women, waiting to pelt their foes with eggs and choice insults: 'Ruffian, jeva chokra...'

An archival photo of Cusrow Baug

My brother didn't mind the splattering eggs and comparison to ruffians. I did. So we usually took the long route home. Past the stone offices and courtyards of the Bombay Electric Supply and Transport Company, from where horse-drawn trams once rattled on their way to Pydhonie. And later electric trams and red BEST buses chuntered through the city, past miniature Wesley Church.

Wesley Church is a small stone affair that truly belongs to a bucolic English village. As a toddler, I had attended Mrs Shellim's Nursery School in its bleak interiors, amidst plaques commemorating the dear departed:

To the Memory of
The Rev G. W. Clutterbuck
First minister of this Church (1886-1890)
Who laboured with untiring energy and devotion
For the establishment of Wesleyan Methodism in Bombay.
The courage and self-sacrifice which marked his life
Were conspicuous in his dying hour
He perished in the wreck of the SS Stella
Near the Channel Islands
March 30th 1899

Maud Emily Edwards
Who entered on Higher Service
20th December 1909
Her life's dream had been to come to India in obedience to her Master's call.
After fifteen month's work and worship here, having nursed her husband, the minister of this church through a dangerous illness, she quietly passed away.
Her body lies in the churchyard at Igatpuri.

It's fortunate that I was too little then to read these doleful postcards from the past. But I do remember sunlight filtering through jewel-bright diamonds of glass. And magnificent Mrs Shellim, whose Baghdadi Jewish descent and lavender-rinsed hair—coiffed with twists, curls and pearls—elevated her to a genuine Colaba character.

If we had walked straight on from Wesley Church, we would have reached the strip of Arabian Sea that separates the island city from the mainland. Instead, we turned onto

Colaba Causeway, with its shoppers, hawkers and ice-lolly-lickers. Here there were psychedelic pastries to ogle, and pink plastic earrings shaped like telephones. Not to forget the well-thumbed Mills and Boon romances displayed at the circulating library run out of a vast metal box on the footpath of the busy main road. *Five Go on an Adventure, Summer Term at St Clare's, A Greek Summer, Purple Passion, The Far Pavilions*—they marked the growth of several generations of Colabaites, just as surely as the 10-paisa weighing scale at Paradise Restaurant.

The bells of the 200-year-old Bhid Bhanjan Mahadev Mandir clanged as we turned towards home. From where, while slugging that non-negotiable glass of tepid milk, I looked down on the wide, wise banyan tree that hosted a long-tailed paradise flycatcher and blue kingfisher. And beyond this avian adda, at a dilatory gulmohar.

This foolish gulmohar tree stood by an old stone wall in Cusrow Baug. It bloomed in the first week of June—a full month after its friends and family across Bombay—and then looked woebegone as its blossoms splatted to the ground with the first gusts of the monsoon. Beyond its branches lay the grey triangle of the Arabian Sea with its promise of exotic elsewheres.

It irked me that I couldn't accept its invitation. That my life seemed limited to this narrow strip of land, dotted with palm trees and edged with lighthouses. All my friends lived next door. My grandparents lived down the road in a vast apartment overlooking the Taj Mahal Hotel. Dr Badshah and his sticky red syrups were six sneezes away. Even our towel-and-bucket acquisition sprees were restricted to the local, pipe-festooned hardware store that went by the unlovely name of Fagniya, to the inevitably out-of-stock halls of Sahakari Bhandar and to Salim's father's plastic shop.

Dull though these sorties were, they came with bonuses: warm jalebis from Kailash Parbat; a pair of silver earrings from the unexpectedly trendy jewellery shops in the bazaar; a morsel of juicy gossip. For there were always Colaba characters afoot.

Firoza Lalli, the famously dotty ballet teacher of Cusrow Baug, with her frizzy hair, twisted feet and tragic story. J.J. Rodriguez, the dapper ballroom-dance teacher, who always looked like he had stepped out of a black-and-white Hollywood film. Meenakshi, the sultry Koli fisherwoman, who was rumoured to have had three baskets of gold stashed in her seaside hut. Mummy and Mamma Wilson and their foster daughters (one of whom—perhaps because of her golden-brown ringlets and Middle-Eastern name—was said to be an Arab princess hidden away from kidnappers).

We monitored the unlikely romance between the Binny Emporium salesman and the Ramlila saleslady. And the dark-and-stormy night crimes that shook our placid neighbourhood. Years later, our corner of Colaba was jolted when the very same Ramlila saleswoman—a hatchet-faced woman who sold me my first Maidenform bra—was brutally murdered amidst boxes of lingerie in that narrow, cluttered shop. The newspapers reported that she had been a Bahai.

The police said that she had been a victim of a random act of violence. Her family disagreed. Yet another Colaba mystery fated to remain unsolved.

But this was at least ten years in the future. The Ramlila saleswoman was still romancing her improbable swain when I was a schoolgirl dragging my feet down the Causeway: stopping every few steps to smile at aunties, cobblers, petrol pump attendants; and fielding the inevitable question: 'How are you, Baby?'

I took the affection and the baby status for granted. I wished my mother would hurry. I wanted to get away from the cosiness and nosiness of Colaba. To Mallory Towers. To Riverdale. To lands across the Arabian Sea.

So it was only much later—in another city by another sea—that I realized how closely I was linked to this rocky headland. Hornblende and feldspar, padded with palm leaves and fish bones, blanketed by asphalt. A once-island lapped by a sea the colour of old school socks.

I spent two years in Los Angeles, working towards my Master's degree. Then everyone around me began seeking jobs and apartments in Pomona, Pasadena, Wichita. I didn't.

For whenever I thought about the future, my imagination hurtled ahead of me to this neighbourhood, so open to waves, winds and ideas. To the rain bouncing off the tiled roofs of Cusrow Baug. To the flowers plopping wetly from that foolish tree, its branches shaking in the wind and beckoning me back to my 400005 pin code.

(Colaba Lesson for Life—All that glitters is not home.)

2. Colabaites, Colabawalas, Colabakars

'Pearl Padamsee lived in Belha Terrace. I spent over a year there rehearsing two plays, The Serpent *and* Godspell. *We performed* The Serpent *in the Scot's Kirk, wearing leotards. It wasn't easy to get leotards those days. I had a pair with some jungle print which were then dyed black. After many performances our leotards all had holes in them, so we coloured in our skin with eyebrow pencil. It was a lot of fun and a bit edgy. There were only two senior actors in the play, plus one slightly older couple…the rest of us were seventeen-year-olds. And, of course, there was Pearl presiding over it all.*

'Colaba has always had so many facets and quite a lot of "characters". Old Edward the VIII and new Theobroma. Tata Textiles, then Health and Glow, now Samsonite or Delsey I guess and/or Nike and Adidas… The little Goan eating places, the art galleries. I remember an artist who literally lived in a garret and painted mostly nudes. His name was Nelson, which

he spelt Nailsun. Then there was another guy whom we called The Walker. He was a mystery figure who was everywhere. You would be driving, he would be walking, and still he seemed to be ahead. I was very let down to find out that he actually had a name, a life and a family.'

—Sherree Carlos, a Colaba lover who was born in Badhwar Park, later shifted to the Brady's Flats and experienced a 'rather vivid kind of growing up' between two bits of water.

GULMOHAR TREES WERE GREAT FAVOURITES THROUGH MY childhood. Their blazing orange flowers were harbingers of summer holidays and freedom. They dolloped hope and colour onto the greyest corners of the city. It seems unfair that they've fallen from grace. As have the other 'exotics' that are so much a part of our everydays—the copper pod, with its yellow flowers; the rain tree, with its delicate pink blooms. Unlike the hardy native trees, we are told, these incomers have shallow roots that won't adapt to local conditions. These migrants from distant shores, apparently, provide neither shelter nor food to local birds and insects.

Still, it's impossible to think of these trees as undesirable aliens. They are as much a part of our lives as the bhelpuri of Kailash Parbat, the eccentrics of Cusrow Baug, the 'Funky Town' blasting from terrace parties. All from elsewhere, all hardcore Colabakars.

The copper pod came to Mumbai from Malaysia and Indonesia. Every summer it carpets the streets with exuberant yellow. The gulmohar—gul is the Persian word for flower and mohar means peacock—is a native of Madagascar. It arrived in India around 1840 via Mauritius. Come summer, it turns into a blazing beauty—the flamboyant peacock of the botanical world.

The rain tree with its powderpuff flowers is originally from Brazil and Mexico. The British brought this quick-growing tree to India as a source of railway firewood. For years I imagined that its name came from its umbrella-shaped crown. But the true reason is quirkier. The rain tree is a favourite with insects like aphids, which excrete a sugary waste called honeydew. The honeydew drizzles down and confuses passers-by. Every evening, this tree folds its leaves and goes to sleep till dawn—which explains its Tamil name, thoongomoonji maram, or 'sleepyhead tree'.

At the very edge of Colaba, outside the National Gallery of Modern Art, stands a landmark rain tree that provides shade to chaiwalas, keychain-sellers and name-on-a-grain-of-rice-writers. Elsewhere in Colaba are venerable gulmohars and copper pods that grow alongside the fluttering pipals and ample banyans. It seems churlish to resent these familiar friends just because they were once outsiders. After all, in Colaba, almost all of us were once outsiders.

My great-grandfather, Nomanbhoy Abdeali, for example, was a Surat boy who made his fortune in the Far East. Then he decided that it was time to get his three daughters married and transplanted them from Singapore to the Bombay of the late 1920s. He moved into an apartment in Sargent House, a handsome, red-brick building off Colaba Causeway—around the same time that the gulmohars and copper pods arrived in the area.

The story of Sargent House and its twin, Jenkins House, runs parallel to the history of Colaba. Like its better-known neighbours—the Yacht Club, the Taj Mahal Hotel and the Gateway of India—Sargent House sits on land that was once swamp and sea. Like them, it is part of the brick-and-mortar skeleton around which Colaba flourished.

For most of its life, Colaba was a rocky wilderness that attracted neither residents not visitors. Then in 1838, a causeway was built to connect the two southernmost islands—Colaba and Old Woman's Island—to the rest of busy Bombay. In 1860, the entire expanse between the Apollo Bunder promenade and the causeway was reclaimed. The 43 acres were used not just for clubs and hotels, but for solid, comfortable buildings that set the tone for this new neighbourhood.

Jamsetji Tata, the legendary industrialist and philanthropist who founded the Tata group of companies, was among those who saw the potential of this freshly minted land. Even before he built the Taj Mahal Hotel, he constructed a string of buildings that he marketed to the new class of Englishmen streaming into Bombay—the bankers, merchants and traders, dismissively dubbed 'boxwallahs' by their compatriots. With this target audience in mind, Tata named the buildings after prominent Englishmen in the city. 'On an individual level he remained a warm friend to scores of Englishmen, including several judges of the Bombay High Court,' wrote R.M. Lala in *For the Love of India: The Life and Times of Jamsetji Tata*. 'It is not accidental that the buildings he had built behind the Taj—before the hotel came up—were named after Englishmen. Reay House, Roosevelt House, Sargent House, Sandhurst House, Jenkins House and Candy House.'

It seems fitting that Nomanbhoy Abdeali should have chosen a home that had so recently risen from the sea, alongside other outsiders who were gradually becoming insiders. Together, these diverse, extraordinary individuals were fashioning the quiet but rich story of Colaba.

In Sargent House there lived Dr Ramaiah Naidu, who had worked with Marie Curie and helped set up the Tata Memorial Hospital. And his daughter, the radiant Leela Naidu, who was featured in *Vogue*'s list of the ten most beautiful women in the world and who acted in a handful of acclaimed movies, including *Yeh Raste Hain Pyar Ke*. This was based on that most romanticized of Colaba killers—Kawas Nanavati, the naval officer who shot his wife's lover in cold-blood and was then portrayed as a hero by the tabloids. Leela Naidu played the half-French wife who strays.

Later, Leela Naidu married poet and writer Dom

Moraes, who brought creative genius to this patch of Colaba. In *The Solitude of Emperors*, David Davidar talks of 'Dom hammering away with one finger at his typewriter in Sargent House, spectacles slipping down his nose as the poems ran wild in his head.' Others recall the late-night salons at No. 17, Sargent House, where inspiration and liquor flowed in equal measure.

The heritage building was also home to Mickey Correa and Lucila Pacheco, who were part of the swing bands at the Taj and other Colaba hotels. Then there was Harry Lyttler, the disciplinarian but brilliant British piano teacher, who stayed back in Bombay—along with his two grand and two upright pianos—even after India became independent. His students included Leela Naidu and painter Mehlli Gobhai.

Then there was cricketer Rusi Modi, and Jalabala Vaidya, who became internationally famous as a stage actor—especially for her rendition of the Ramayana, in which she played all twenty-two characters.

As a child, I visited Sargent House often, and remember it for the grand Bohra feasts and unique, two-door elevator. My daughters know it too. For—in the kind of coincidence that only Colaba throws up—my brother and his family now live in a Tata Institute of Fundamental Research flat on the ground floor of Sargent House. My brother is a string theorist who spent many years in freezing, faraway cities. So, it's incredible that he should find himself just three floors beneath the house that our great-grandfather moved into almost a century ago.

This is especially ironic because, of the three sisters who came to Mumbai from Singapore, my grandmother Meryam was the one who moved away. Even though it was just down the road.

Soon after coming to Bombay, my grandmother was married into a family of Indian National Congress supporters who lived a few minutes away. Crescent House stood on Colaba Causeway and it was in a long, narrow apartment on the top floor that my grandmother learnt to swap soft Chinese silks for khadi; to cope with the death of her first husband and to bring up her little daughter by herself. While outside her window, Colaba Causeway rumbled with electric trams, brash electric lights replaced the flicker of gaslights, and adventurers with secrets and women with pasts arrived from every continent.

My grandmother must have looked down on the same Colaba as did Joe Mummery on the pages of *Soldier of Misfortune*. This boxing novel, written by P.C. Wren, is clichéd and dated but offers a rare snapshot of the Bombay of the 1920s. Josephus Mummery has just arrived on *HMS Tenerife* and from the Seaman's Rest—today the office of the Director General of Police near the Museum—he observes the 'kaleidoscopic mosaic' unfolding before his weary eyes: 'Bullock carts plied between the bunders and the Colaba cotton yards and the ticca gharries between the Yacht Club, Watson's Hotel, the Great Western Hotel, the Apollo Hotel and the Great Indian Peninsula Railway. In brilliant coloured turbans and coats, or saris and petticoats, went Mussalman and Hindu, man and woman of every race of India, as well as Arab, Chinese, Persian, Negro, Afghan, Cingalee, Burman, Jap and Russian, Turk, Jew and Infidel.'

The Colaba of the 1930s was lively, even risqué. Every day steamers arrived from Karachi, dhows from Africa, ships from England—filled with men and women seeking excitement and fortune in those brittle, unsettled decades between the World Wars. 'In those days,' wrote Louis Bromfield in *Night in Bombay*, 'Bombay was a wide open town. The Taj Mahal, like the Raffles Hotel in Singapore and the Hotel des Indes in Batavia, was a famous rendezvous for men and women from all over the East. They came from Sumatra and Macassar and the Malay States, from Medan Deli and Samarang and Borneo and Ceylon and Sourabaya.'

Tyebjee Barma, my other great-grandfather, was one of those who journeyed through the East. As the chief accountant of a vast trading company and later as a businessman, he lived in Hong Kong, Shanghai and Kobe—but he maintained a base in Bombay. My grandfather was the son who handled affairs in India. He was a widower with a young son.

The self-appointed matchmakers of the Bohra Muslim community—as alert a bunch of busybodies as you will ever find—must have spotted the symmetry and gotten cracking. My grandfather and grandmother got married and some years later moved into Sunny House, opposite the Taj Mahal Hotel.

That was where my mother grew up. From where she walked to St Anne's School. And later, from where she hurried every morning to catch the red 6 Ltd bus that would take her off the island of Colaba to the Haffkine Research Institute on the island of Parel.

It so happened that there was a newcomer in the area. A young Parsi cricketer from Hyderabad who lived in one of the not-entirely-salubrious guesthouses that dotted the side streets. Every morning he too hurried to the bus stop to catch a red 6 Ltd bus to his office in Byculla. Gradually, he noticed a girl with long hair and a serious expression. The young Hyderabadi hero was an ardent follower of Hindi cinema so, of course, he knew just what to do. He dropped a book. Then he concocted a sister who wanted to study medicine. He started a conversation—and if you've watched even half a Bollywood movie, you know exactly where this is heading.

Of course, there was stiff opposition, as there is in the best blockbusters. Even so, the academic Bohra girl and the Parsi hero got married. I was born a couple of years later—the product of Colaba serendipity.

We moved into Batra House on Sorab Bharucha Road in 1975. Like Sargent House had fifty years ago, the story of Batra House revealed a new chapter in the story of Colaba.

Sorab Bharucha was a prominent architect. Mr Batra was a refugee who had made his way from Sind to Bombay in 1947. This was a time when the authorities were trying to generate housing for the refugees streaming into Bombay. They spotted a small, irregular garden at the end of a lane lined with the handsome, grey Brady's Flats, built in 1920 for the officers of the Brady's Mills, located near Sassoon Dock. The authorities decreed that the garden was a frivolity the city could do without. The land went to Mr Batra.

A slew of quick, blocky buildings were rising from the vacant plots near Colaba Bazaar. Mr Batra's five-storeyed structure was part of this brave 'Little Sind'. It was irregularly shaped, like the garden it replaced. The crooked little apartments were snapped up by a few Sindhi families and a Parsi family that had left Pakistan. A Catholic family moved into the ground floor.

One of the apartments on the fourth floor was sold to a singer named Mohammed Rafi, who was just stepping into the world of Hindi cinema. His mellifluous voice floated through the building every morning when he did his riyaz. Just as it floated over the radio some years later, filling the building and streets outside with 'Gun guna rahe hai bhawre' and 'Khoya khoya chand'.

That was the apartment that my parents bought in a lane full of heritage buildings with names like Linden House and Johnson House. Coincidentally—but then, Colaba is full of happenstance—Mrs Shellim of the purple hair and nursery school lived three buildings away. So did my needlework teacher from Fort Convent. And if you know anything about girls' schools and needlework, you will know that needlework teachers are the most fearsome of them all.

It was from this perch on the fourth floor that I peered at the Arabian Sea and wondered where I would wash up if I swam and swam in a straight line (Oman. Not the answer I was hoping for. Perhaps that was the reason I never learnt to swim.)

It was also from here that my brother and I goggled when a bedroom window mysteriously cracked and splintered one summer afternoon. I thought it had been pecked by a crow, till we found three air-gun pellets and realized that it had been shot by a fruitcake teenager living across from us in Cusrow Baug. (He still lives there, by the way—now a father of two, who complains about noise and stands at his window, frowning under beetling brows.)

How do I know? Because I still live in Batra House. Three floors below the apartment that my parents bought.

Of course, I ventured a long way from Colaba—to Los Angeles first and to Dadar next, close to the heart of Mumbai. I liked being in the middle of things. But when my husband suggested that we head back to Colaba, I agreed with alacrity.

My three daughters are Colaba girls. So are the characters in many of the books I write for children. Nivi and Sarita in *The Six Spellmakers of Dorabji Street* save two bimbli trees in a Colaba garden. The very two trees that I climbed as a twelve-year-old, but couldn't save in real life. Maya in *What Maya Saw* lives in a boxy building near Colaba Bus Station, where she is visited by creepy baddies. Nimmi—who has a series of her very own—lives in a soulless skyscraper in Cuffe Parade.

The Colaba in which they are growing up is not all that different from the Colaba in which I grew up. In some ways, it is still the snug world that Pearl Padamsee, actor, director and Colaba-lover, wrote about in 1982: 'There was a time when my daughter used to say, "When you go shopping down Colaba, Ma, don't forget to give everybody my love." And I would nod reassuringly, confident of meeting friends and neighbours, exchanging views on this and that, gupshupping on the latest shoe sale or the price of fresh crabs. For Colaba was the scene.'

Grand Bazaar on Colaba Causeway, a newspaper cutting.

Of course, forty years have trundled by. Pearl Padamsee has passed on. The flat in Kulsum Terrace—where Padamsee family performances evolved over the years into professional theatre and where so many of the city's plays have been born and rehearsed, including *Jesus Christ Superstar*, *Godspell*, *Death of a Salesman* and *Romeo and Juliet*—is now just another shabby commercial building along the Causeway.

As you look around the walls, vast 8' by 10' portrait paintings look down at you. On one side is a picture of my mother sitting on a chair with my brother Bobby perched on the arm. On the other side is a picture of my parents in a kind of wedding pose. Then there are portraits of my maternal grandparents and paternal grandparents. These are rather traditional portraits. In those days nobody smiled for a portrait. They all looked rather severe.

But yet, there were two paintings side by side that were always smiling. One was the Aga Khan (whom I had seen weighed in diamonds at the CCI Club). And the other was Lord Krishna. It says something for communal harmony in those days.

*

As the family got more and more involved in the theatre, the cast of each play became an extended family to us. It was social as well as work-oriented. In the great cause of culture we were creating something together. So there was much laughter, music, dancing and falling in love. In fact, my first three sisters all married into the Theatre Group.

—From Alyque Padamsee's memoir, *Double Life*,
an extract about his home on Colaba Causeway.
Padamsee's father built Kulsum Terrace in the 1930s
using Italian marble, mosaic tiles and fancy fittings, and
named it after his wife Kulsumbai.

Binny has vanished and so has Ramlila. So have Salim, his father and their shop that sold buckets, boxes and a jumble of plastic caps, waiting for the perfect bottle to whisk them away.

Somewhere along the way, Bombay has become Mumbai. We see a few more namaaz topis and orange flags around Colaba Bazaar. A few more chalk-and-blackboard notices at the gate of Cusrow Baug that announce the passing of yet another resident of this dwindling community.

But not everything has changed. Colaba remains breezy, briny and somewhat eccentric. The gulmohar tree in Cusrow Baug procrastinates as much as ever. You still get pink plastic earrings on Colaba Causeway—only now they are shaped like mobile phones. And even today, as I hurry along, I encounter that familiar greeting. 'How are you, Baby?'

This time around, I'm grateful for the cosiness, the nosiness; the affection and the eternal baby status. This time around, I don't hurry away.

(Colaba Lesson for Life—Quick! Talk to your grandparents before it's too late.)

3. Geography

'Our house was built as a beach house on the rocky sea front. When I was young, there was even a long rowing boat lying in the loft of our garage. By the time I was born, though, the road had been built in front of the house and the sea had gone.

'When we were in school, the Cuffe Parade reclamation was taking place and we used to cycle there. I remember watching the first Cuffe Parade building coming up.'

—Sakib Maskati was born in the Northcote Nursing Home across from the Taj, and grew up in one of the last bungalows in Colaba. This little house, built some time before 1906, is tucked away in a narrow lane behind Colaba Post Office.

'A lot has changed, of course. When I was young there was the road outside our house and then mangroves, mud and sea. There was a big footpath in the middle of the mangroves and some sand like a little Chowpati. I had an ayah who used to pick up white shells, cut them and eat the sea creatures inside.

She said they were delicious. It was very lovely then, and there was no dust.'

—Ziya Maskati, Sakib's aunt, has watched the sea move further and further away from her house over her ninety-two years.

THE IDEA OF THIS BOOK CAME UP OVER GRILLED SANDWICHES and iced tea. My editor was visiting from Delhi. We agreed to meet at a kitschy café with a décor featuring Marilyn Monroe and cheery ceramic tiles. In the interest of poetic justice, I wish I could say that the café was in Colaba. In the interest of journalistic accuracy, I have to admit that it was not.

This book was born in Kala Ghoda, which is almost, almost Colaba. But not quite. Two hundred years ago, the journey from Colaba to Kala Ghoda would have involved a tedious, time-consuming ferry ride. Perhaps it's that lingering memory that gives the areas their distinctness. And not even I—greedy for Ropewalk Lane and a powder-blue synagogue with white trim—can pretend that Kala Ghoda is part of my territory.

Or Rampart Row where, on Table No. 4 of Wayside Inn, Dr Babasaheb Ambedkar wrote chunks of the Indian Constitution. Or Lion's Gate, where the mahogany tree, planted by the famous explorer Dr David Livingstone in 1865, still spreads it branches.

Or Rajabai Clock Tower with sculptures and embellishments overseen by Sir Lockwood Kipling, father of Rudyard Kipling. Though the reason I want to sneak the clock tower into this book has nothing to do with architecture or 'If', and has everything to do with that sunny evening in 1891 when Bachubai and Pherozebai—the wife and sister of Ardeshir Godrej—tumbled to their deaths from the clock tower. Murder, suicide or accident? The mystery was never solved. For although the finger of suspicion pointed at a wily and wealthy individual named Manekji Aslaji, he escaped scot free with the assistance of his valet Bala, a corrupt English policeman and a vanished coat. And the fact that the married Bachubai happened to be a virgin.

Rajabai Clock Tower and Rampart Row may not belong in a book on Colaba, but then what does? At what precise point does my neighbourhood slide into someone else's neighbourhood? Where do the boundaries lie?

Maybe, I decide, the Municipal Corporation will know. Or even the police. But after innumerable wasted hours, it's apparent that these bastions of bureaucracy have divvied up the city based on convenience rather than local history, and neither ward limits nor police jurisdictions are of much use.

Which is when I decide to peer into the past. After all, Mumbai was once a scatter of seven islands in the Arabian Sea. The island of Colaba was one of that emerald cluster. All I need to do is locate that island of 150 years ago beneath the paving stones and traffic jams, cement and skyscrapers. How difficult can that be? The short answer is very, very difficult. For the long answer, read on.

The journey into the past begins on a predictable note. Like any other neophyte researcher, I turn to *The Gazetteer of Bombay City and Island* written in 1909 by the prolific and erudite S.M. Edwardes. The book provides a wealth of historical detail and meticulously describes the seven islands that the Portuguese and English happened upon in the 16th century.

Straggly, marshy Parel, lush with tamarind and prickly pear trees. This island was dotted with hamlets and settlements dating from the time of Raja Bimb in the 14th century. Next to it was Mahim, flat, low and prosperous. Tucked away among its palms were the famed temple of Prabhadevi and the tomb of Sheikh Ali Paru. Then the rocky ledge of Worli, once separated from the island of Bombay by a great breach through which the sea poured in at high tide with 'all the fury and pleasure of an Arabian colt'. Beneath these three northern islands was the large, central island of Bombay, shaped like an H, covered with tropical jungles and rimmed with rocks. This island extended from Malabar Hill on the west to Dongri on the east and had a sprinkling of Koli settlements, a thriving village and fields prone to flooding. Perched above Bombay was the small island of Mazagaon, 'part hill, part dale'. It was separated from the mother island by Umarkhadi or the Creek of the Fig Tree. South of this, on the other side of a fairly wide strait, was a tiny triangle known to the Portuguese as Al Omanis and to the British by the rather more sinister name of Old Woman's Island. And then, finally, the mangroves and narrow tongue of rock upon which perched the huts of a few Koli fishermen: Colaba.

Satisfied with this predictable picture of the past, I don my spectacles and peer at old maps. Which is when I walk slap-bang into obstacles, quite as rocky as the islands I'm hoping to excavate.

I start with the 'Map of Bombay Showing Islands As They Existed in 1670'. This is a familiar piece of cartography, one that pops up alongside any article about Bombay's history. It depicts seven tiny amoeba-shaped blobs. A skeleton so rickety and disjointed that it's impossible to imagine that a megapolis will rise over and around its feeble bones.

So far, so good.

The next map I examine is Fryer's Map, which dates back to 1672 and, as I peer at it, I'm puzzled. This map was executed by John Fryer who was a doctor with the East India Company and enjoyed writing about his travels. It has the hasty, approximate air of a map sketched by a pizza delivery boy on the back of a bill. Clearly, John Fryer could not have imagined that this map would go down in posterity. Even so, it's peculiar that there's absolutely no correlation between the Bombay of 1670 and the Bombay of 1672.

Fryer has depicted the top of Bombay as a squat, fat blob. This is separated by a channel of water from a little tail of land that he identifies as Old Woman's Island. 'These islands are in number seven,' he wrote. 'Bombay, Canorein, Trumbay, Elephanto, the Putachoes, Munchumbay and Kerenjan, with the rock of Henery Kenery; arising as so many mountains out of the sea.'

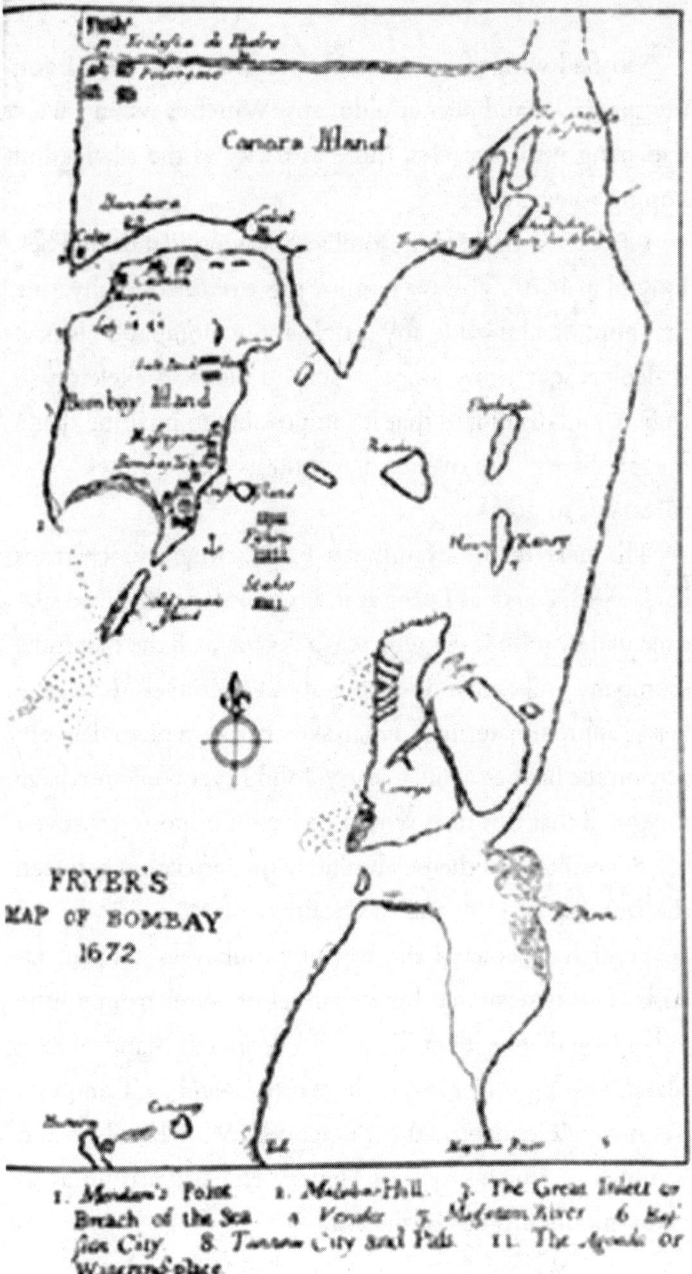

John Fryer's Map of the Bombay of 1672.
Source: Wikimedia Commons.

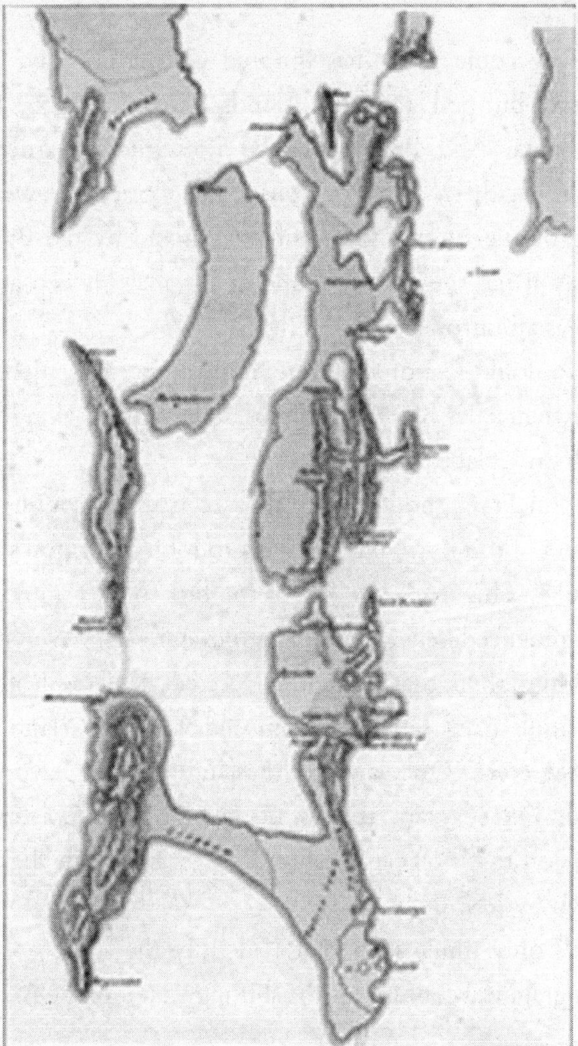

A Map of the Island of Bombay and Colaba prepared in 1843. *Source: Wikimedia Commons.*

How come Fryer has ignored Colaba entirely? And instead bunged random islands into the mix? Like Elephanta. And Putachoes—the Portuguese 'garden of melons' with its desirable houses and glorious views was later tongue-twisted into Butcher's Island by the British. Today it has the prosaic name of Jawahar Dweep and is used as an unromantic oil terminal.

No doubt Canorein, Munchumbay and Kerenjen also have their tales to tell, but those tales don't belong in a book on Colaba.

'John Fryer should have stuck to treating coughs and cholera,' I think snippily as I turn to John Thornton's map of 1685. This map was one of the first to be printed and has influenced generations of cartographers. It's even more boggling, then, that Thornton, too, has depicted Bombay as a single mass, separated from Old Woman's Island by a narrow creek. Once again, the islands seem to have been fused. Once again, there's no mention of Colaba—an omission that's repeated a hundred years later in the map drawn by J.N. Bellin in 1750.

It's only much later that I identify the source of this cartographical confusion—the shifting waters of the Arabian Sea.

For while none of the maps have lied, none have revealed the truth. In fact, even the assertion that Bombay is made up of seven islands teeters between fact and fiction. It is part of what Tim Riding—in 'Making Bombay Island:

Land Reclamation and Geographical Conceptions of Bombay, 1661–1728'—described as a 'web of myth and misconception' that has grown over the centuries.

The archipelago that lay alongside the north Konkan coast in the 1600s comprised around twenty-five islands. A group of these sat close together and shared a peculiar kinship. In the *Gazetteer*, Edwardes explains that these islands were separated by a 'fairly wide, shallow creek, into which the seas around poured during the high tides and flooded the low-lying stretches of all islands'.

The relationship between the islands was in constant flux. At low tide, it was sometimes possible to walk from one island to another. At high tide, a boat was imperative. 'At the centre of this confusion is the issue of how to define the archipelago's topography,' wrote Riding, pointing out that the land between the islands was 'neither sea nor land, but something in between'.

Whether Bombay was a single mass of land or a cluster of islands depended on the beholder, and the crown to which he or she pledged allegiance. So while the Portuguese perceived a group of independent islands, the English saw a single land mass—which makes perfect sense if you put yourselves in the leather boots of those 17th-century colonialists.

As the textbooks never tire of telling us, Charles II of England married Catherine of Braganza and received the island of Bombay as part of her dowry in 1662. What they don't tell us, however, is that the transfer of this gift was far from amicable or straightforward.

When Charles II's emissaries came to claim the king's portion, there were already Portuguese families living the good life and loath to give up their lush gardens, manors and top-dog status. They resented the fact that they were pawns in a game of matrimonial chess and, unwilling to oblige the royal English son-in-law, clung onto every inch of land they possibly could.

When the British arrived in 1664, there was already some uncertainty. Charles II—who by all accounts was a distracted ruler—had lost the map that provided the details of his dowry. This led to bitter bargaining between the Portuguese and British. The Portuguese defined Bombay as the single, central island of Bombay. Period. The British, in turn, insisted that Bombay included Worli, Parel, Mahim and Mazagaon. They ignored the fact that people regularly travelled from one island to the other by boat, and rubbished the claim that the sea separated Bombay from Parel, or Parel from Mahim. Instead, they described the space between the islands as 'drowned land' or 'waste land' or 'the flats'.

'The first act of Mr Humphrey Cooke, who is the Governor of that island and whom I knew in Lisbon as a grocer, was to take possession of the island of Mahim in spite of my protests, the island being some distance from the island of Bombay, as your Majesty will see from the map I send herewith,' a fulminating Antonio de Mello de

Castro, the Viceroy of Portugal, wrote to his king in 1666. 'He argues that at low tide one can walk from one end to the other, and if this is conceded, your Majesty will be unable to defend the right to the other northern islands, as at low tide it is possible to go from Bombay to Salsette, from Salsette to Varagaon, so that in order not to lose the north, it will be necessary to defend Mahim.'

It makes perfect sense now that Fryer, Thornton and gang depicted Bombay, Parel, Mahim, Worli and Mazagaon as a single land mass. They were merely toeing the official line. Only Old Woman's Island and Colaba were considered separate entities—both by the Portuguese and the British.

The answer to one mystery, however, throws up another. If the colonial powers were determined to see Bombay as a single land mass, how and when did the seven islands emerge from those layers of administrative obfuscation? And what about that mysterious 'Map of Bombay Showing Islands As They Existed in 1670'? Who put that together, and when?

Tim Riding believes that in the early 19th century, the British started taking an interest in local history. They were startled to find that Marathi storytellers and texts often described Mahim and Bombay as separate islands. Intrigued, Robert Murphy, an editor and translator, conducted his own research and decided that Bombay was made up of four islands. Along with Colaba and Old Woman's Island, this made a total of six. After studying old documents, listening to the traditional tales and pondering over the names of places, Murphy prepared a map. The Bombay Geographical Society used it as a basis for its own version—'constructed from actual surveys and documents of old date in the office of the Collector of Land Revenue'—and came up with an official map that showed seven islands.

So, incredible as it seems, the map that depicts the Bombay of 1670—the basis of so many of our assumptions about the city—was actually drawn in the 19th century. Even stranger, it was created out of poetry and memories rather than observation and measurement.

Still, the idea of seven islands snagged the imagination. From here it was but a short leap to the conclusion that the seven islands of Bombay were the seven islands of Ptolemy's Heptanesia. And, just like that, Bombay acquired for itself a pedigreed past. One that was passed on to the little girls of Fort Convent and the little boys of Campion School; one that has made its way to the Bournvita Quiz Contest and *Encyclopedia Britannica* and Wikipedia; one that has become incontrovertible fact.

Through the twists and turns of this tale, however, two patches of land retained their island status: Old Woman's Island and Colaba.

Old Woman's Island was a smallish mound—a stepping-stone between Bombay and Colaba. It was separated from the island of Bombay by a wide strait, and from Colaba by a narrow inlet that filled with water during the high tide.

But where exactly did these fickle, watery boundaries run? Where did one island end and another begin?

First-hand accounts indicate that the little creek dividing Colaba and Old Woman's Island ran from the north of Sassoon Dock to the front of Colaba Station, where once the BB and CI Railway deposited passengers and great bales of cotton. Sassoon Dock remains where it always was. But Colaba Station is gone. It popped up often during conversations with my grandfather as a vague but fond memory. I never asked him exactly where it stood. I wish I had.

The precise location of Colaba Station, when I finally track it down, is both logical and startling. Logical because Colaba Station once stood where Badhwar Park, a colony for railway officers and their families, stands today. Startling because Badhwar Park is my immediate neighbour. Its mundane, red and white buildings have always been part of the view outside my window. It is difficult to imagine that beneath this prosaic reality lies the subject of so many vintage photographs: a gothic structure of sloping roofs, arched windows and turrets, sitting alone under a big sky and gazing at a big sea. Like the housing colony that replaced it, this station too wore an air of permanence. And it seems unlikely that the passengers who passed through its arched porch—including my grandfather and his friends, who once hopped onto a train to Surat without informing their families—imagined that very soon the station would be the stuff of unreliable recollections.

At the moment though, I'm interested in what lies beneath the stone station—and try to conjure up a patch of wilderness sloping into a creek. There are no details about when this little inlet became land; when Old Woman's Island was swallowed up by Colaba. All we know is that today, an untidy clutter of mithai bhandars and frock shops stand where once was water. Delighted that one geographical mystery is resolved, I turn to the next.

The broad strait that separated Old Woman's Island and the island of Bombay was a prominent feature of the city till 1838. It claimed lives and caused enormous inconvenience. It was the reason why Colaba was the ultimate boondocks. 'The breach between Colaba and Old Woman's Island was not formidable and was only covered by the sea at high tide,' wrote Samuel Sheppard in *Bombay*. 'Between Old Woman's Island and Mendham's Point on Bombay Island there was a deep channel, which in later years could be crossed on a ferry boat worked with a rope.'

But where, precisely, did this channel run? Sheppard offers an answer: 'A stone in the Colaba Police Station compound now marks the place from which the ferry was worked, and, according to the inscription on that stone, the channel was 300 yards across. At low water it was possible to ride across it; but that, as more than one accident showed, was not a safe after-dinner amusement.'

In a city that scores so low in the historical landmarks department, the thought of this stone is compelling. A couple of days later, I walked through the arched gate of the Colaba Police Station and wandered around, trying not to look skulky or suspicious. I spent ten minutes nosing around the compound and its bushes, by which point it was glaringly obvious that I was not here for passport verification. Somehow, I'd assumed that the marker would be easy to find. It was not. I'd assumed that selfie-taking tourists and signposts would lead the way. They didn't. Finally, I asked a constable. He shrugged. A second constable pointed to a house in the middle of the compound. 'Ring their doorbell,' he said.

There's something distinctly odd about a house in the middle of a police station. There's something even odder about a rare historical relic being swallowed by this house. Still, I rang the bell. A woman emerged into the cluttered courtyard, but the moment she heard the words 'old stone' she stormed back inside.

Defeated for the moment, I headed back to Colaba Causeway and peered past buses and tourists at the other shore of that long-ago creek. To get there would take me about six minutes, past shops selling embroidered slippers, bubble tea and smoky topaz necklaces. Two hundred years ago, the same journey would have involved a ride in a ferry of 'reeking straw and filth' and 'so badly lighted that passengers were in danger of being drowned'. Passengers would have clambered out of the ferry near Mendham's Point—the British cemetery that claimed unnumbered soldiers and administrators before they could even write their first letter home.

This notorious graveyard was razed in 1762, and its precise location was forgotten. Almost a century later, the Royal Alfred Sailor's Home rose in its place. Then in 1928, workmen began to dig a foundation near the Royal Alfred Sailor's Home and got a nasty shock. 'Workmen came across human bones quite early in their operations and, affrightened less evil spirits should be disturbed, they downed tools,' reported the *Times of India*. 'But they were soon persuaded to resume their work, and day after day they have laid bare more bones.' Later, the stone building became the office of the Director General of Police.

As I stood at the edge of a ghost creek, aquiver with ghost fish, it struck me that much of my world is built on water. Metro Shoe Shop, which my friends and I visited day after day to pine over the ultimate pink stilettos. Delhi Darbar, where we celebrated report cards and birthdays with redolent biryanis and frilly chicken farchas. Fort Convent, where we learnt that Bombay was a city made up of seven islands and that we were on the island of Colaba. Where we learnt that if we performed enough acts of kindnesses, we could change the future. (How many other inaccurate facts were we inadvertently fed?)

Then there was the Ratan Tata Institute, home of sublime lemon rolls and crotchety saleswomen who sloooowly filled our boxes with pastries. Then slooooowly made the bill. And then slowly, slowly, slowly counted out the changed. If we tried to hurry them along, they snapped back in pungent Parsi Gujarati: 'Ghoda par bethi ne aavyach su?' We had to admit that we had not come to the store on a horse. Very few people in the Bombay of the 1980s did. Our defeat was complete.

Sargent House and Sunny House stand on land wrested from the sea during the 1860s. Old and New Cuffe Parade stand on land created within the last 120 years. And somewhere beneath the buildings and reclamation schemes lies the original island of Colaba. Its hillocks flattened, its mangroves buried and its boundaries blurred.

Even if it were possible to locate that scraggy island, what would be the point? By the yardstick of the past, Colaba extends from Prong's Reef to Sassoon Dock. By the same yardstick, my immediate world belongs not to Colaba but to a triangular wodge known by that most unattractive name, Old Woman's Island. Which would make me not a Colabaite or Colabakar, but an Old Womankar.

I refuse.

The Colaba of the present cannot be collapsed into the Colaba of the past. Which means I'm back to the original question: What precisely is Colaba?

Finally, it is the *Gazetteer* that suggests a solution of sorts. 'The Colaba section, which is bounded on the north by the Apollo Bunders and Wodehouse Road and the Wodehouse Overbridge and on the south, east and west by the sea, is divided into Upper and Lower Colaba by an imaginary line drawn across the land at the north wall of St. John's Memorial Church. The former area contains the lunatic asylum, the observatory, the shrine of a Musalman saint and the barracks and quarters of the European garrison; the latter area contains the old Colaba village, various cotton presses, the cotton green, Sassoon Dock and the terminus of the Bombay, Baroda and Central India Railway.'

The Colaba that Edwardes described is an unfamiliar place. Even so, his idea of Colaba overlaps with mine. Give or take a Cuffe Parade, a Wodehouse Overbridge and a lunatic asylum or two. As long as I promise not to appropriate Rajabai Clock Tower or Rampart Row, I guess I can move on to the real questions: How did that little spit of land grow up to become Colaba? What peculiar magic abracadeabra-ed a barren straggle of rock into this happy hodgepodge neighbourhood?

(Colaba Lesson for Life—Don't believe everything they teach you in school.)

4. History of a Little Island

'There was a time when Greater Bombay had 276 fishing villages, but because of industrialization, the creeks got spoilt and the hamlets were lost. From original inhabitants, the Kolis of Mumbai have become invisible inhabitants. The Kolis always had their eyes on the sea. They never looked behind them, which is why they never owned property and have been pushed to the edges.

'The Kolis of Colaba originally came from Alibag and the surrounding villages. There was always movement between the mainland and the islands, because the Kolis traditionally fished in the waters that lie in between. The Kolis of the mainland have always believed that Colaba is an extension of their world.'

—Ganesh Nakhawa is a seventh-generation fisherman. He is from Karanja, just across the water from Colaba. His family fished in the creek and their boats regularly crossed it—often bearing pregnant women on their way to a south Mumbai nursing home to deliver their babies. Nakhawa is an activist and has been working towards 'getting respect back for the Kolis'.

What do we know about the history of Colaba? Almost nothing before the 1600s. And even then, what is available is fragmentary and random. Newspaper reports about jackals sighted and churches built. Travellers' accounts with as much substance as a stray blog post on the Net. The histories of colonialists by colonialists—arbitrary spotlights that fall on the European tea parties and tailorbirds in Colaba, but leave its Indian denizens in impenetrable darkness.

In his 1932 book, *Bombay*, Samuel Sheppard mentioned a writer who introduced his work with the warning that the early history of Bombay is 'sunk deep in the Night of Time'. 'When historians make a beginning like that,' Sheppard quipped, 'one may be sure that there is indeed not much to be said.'

It's inevitable, then, that the writer attempting a history of Colaba will have to blunder about in the dark, hoping to stumble upon a skimpy fact, a lucky guess—even more than the writer seeking knowledge about the other, better-documented parts of Mumbai. Still, there are a few things we do know.

We do know that this 'thin prolongation called Colaba' is made up of fine-grained diorite, composed of feldspar and hornblende. That over time, mangroves and palm trees must have appeared on this rocky strip. That gauzy-winged dragonflies must have dropped in during their multi-generational migration from India to Africa. And that Kolis from the mainland, sufi saints from Baghdad, and sailors on their way to more important ports, somehow washed up here.

Historians believe that it is from the Kolis that Colaba got its name. 'Successive waves of Koli settlers seem to have invaded and occupied the different islands of these archipelagos, and in spite of subsequent occupation by many other settlers in later days, the Kolis have survived in these islands till today,' stated Edwardes in the *Gazetteer*. 'In what localities they precisely built their scattered groups of huts is difficult to say. That they undoubtedly existed in two of the southernmost islands is apparent from the fact they acquired the name of Kolabhat or Kolaba, the Koli estates. Immigrants of a later period gave the smaller of the two islands the name, the island of Al Omanis or deep sea fishermen.'

Although the explanation for Colaba is widely accepted, the more picturesque and awful name of Old Woman's Island threw up a colourful multiple choice. 'A rudely carved red-smeared goddess, a venerable Portuguese dame, a wrinkled fate-reading fisherwoman, an antique mother of harlots, have all been invented to explain the name Old Woman's Island,' said Sheppard in *Bombay Place Names and Street Names*. Sadly, these have been discarded in favour of the more humdrum etymology: Old Woman's Island seems to be a typical British misinterpretation of Al Omanis, the Persian phrase used to describe those who fished in deep waters and ventured further in the direction of Oman.

While the denizens of Colaba and Old Woman's Islands were casting their nets, empires were rising and falling around them. The Mauryas, the Shilharas, the Sultan of Gujarat, all ruled over the northern stretch of the Konkan—and by default, over this cluster of insignificant islands.

It is unlikely, however, that the panjandrums spent much time pondering over this sleepy outpost. The action was clearly elsewhere.

Colaba and its sister islands sat alongside a buzzing waterway. Perhaps they looked on forlornly while ships from distant lands sailed between the more happening ports—from Babylon to Sopara; from Mesopotamia to Chaul. In *The Port of Bombay*, W.R.S. Sharpe wrote that the islands of Bombay, 'populated only by a handful of primitive fisherfolk and husbandsmen, slumbered undisturbed on the bosom of the Indian Ocean while the fame of neighbouring ports—Broach, Sopara, Chaul, Janjira, Kalyan, Thana—spread throughout the East and attracted merchant-adventurers from near and far'.

The tables, though, were soon to be turned. Today, Nalasopara is a drab residential suburb on the western line. Chaul is a two-teashop town along the verdant stretch between Alibag and Kamshet. And those neglected, slumbering islands are Megapolis Mumbai.

After Vasco da Gama made his way to India by sea in 1498, the Portuguese used guns and brutality to snatch control of the trade route. While prowling around the coast, they dropped in on Bombay in 1509 and stocked up on wood and other supplies.

This seemingly innocuous visit was followed by a series of raids. By 1534, Sultan Bahadur Shah of Gujarat—who was facing heat from Emperor Humayun—succumbed to Portuguese pressure. Leaping heedlessly from the frying pan into the fire, he struck an agreement and handed over Bassein and its dependencies to the foreign power. The Island of Bombay, Old Woman's Island and Colaba were part of the package.

The Portuguese divided up their new territory into manors or fiefs. These were then given out—for a small rent—to a favoured few.

The English, meanwhile, were also skulking in the wings. The East India Company was busy in other parts of India—setting up factories and eyeing territory. Determined to break the Portuguese stranglehold on the spice trade, English merchants and mercenaries engaged in a series of battles with the Portuguese between 1612 and 1630. During one of these skirmishes, the English sailors reported that the Portuguese had 'got into a hole called Bombay' to repair their ships. When they arrived in Bombay, however, the Portuguese had left and so, feeling cheated, the Englishmen burnt down a few buildings before sailing away. This tantrum is unremarkable but for a single fact—according to the British Library, it's the first time that Bombay pops up in British records.

After this taster, the East India Company began to eye Bombay—with its enviable natural harbour—and even attempted to buy the island from the Portuguese. So it seemed a gift from heaven that in faraway England, a royal marriage was being planned with all the precision of a mega merger.

Charles II, the King of England, Scotland and Ireland, wanted a rich wife. An array of Spanish, Dutch and German brides were paraded before him but he rudely declared, 'Odd's fish, they are all dull and foggy!' He eventually settled on the Portuguese Infanta, and the advisors of both courts gloated that together they would teach the pesky Dutch a lesson.

There was a hot rumour that the Portuguese would add Goa to the Infanta's dower. Eventually, however, the marriage treaty of 1661 included Bombay and Tangiers. The English rejoiced, even though they didn't know exactly what they had netted. Lord Clarendon, who was then the chancellor, famously exulted over 'the islands of Bombay with the towns and castles therein, which are within a very little distance of Brazil'.

The stage was set for confusion. Sir Abraham Shipman, who had been appointed commander-in-chief of Bombay, left England in 1662 with around 400 soldiers. He clearly expected a wealthy island and a warm welcome. He was disappointed on both counts.

The expedition was under the command of the Lord of

Marlborough and was beset with bad luck from the get-go. First, the ship carrying Sir Shipman went astray and the Portuguese refused to hand Bombay over to anybody else. Then, when Sir Shipman finally arrived, the local Portuguese tried their utmost to block the transfer of what Lord Marlborough dismissed as a 'paltry island'.

In 1663, in his famous diary, Samuel Pepys echoed this disenchantment. Referring to Bombay as a 'poor little island', he complained that the Portuguese had indicated that the various islands were 'all one piece'.

Fed up with hanging around, Lord Marlborough returned to England. Sir Shipman and his '400 and odd men' didn't have that option, however, and were forced to wait out the stalemate at Angadiv, an island off Karwar in north Karnataka. Climate, intemperance and disease took a heavy toll on the troops and, by 1663, there were only 140 men left. Then Shipman himself died.

The obstreperous Portuguese families were finally persuaded to hand Bombay over to Humphrey Cooke, who had been secretary to Sir Shipman. The formal ceremony took place on 18 February 1665 and Cooke made a show of 'taking in his hand earth and stones, entering and walking upon its bastions, putting his hands to the walls'.

All the while, however, there was a fierce debate about what constituted Bombay. The Portuguese maintained that they had to hand over just the central H-shaped island. The English countered that Bombay included Mahim, Mazagaon, Worli and Parel.

Cooke eventually got his way, but was dissatisfied. He complained that although a pleasant enough place, this island yielded little besides a great quantity of coconuts and rice. Part of the problem was that while Cooke was adept at snatching islands, he was lousy at administering them. He made enemies everywhere—and was eventually arrested for fraud and embezzlement. He then escaped to Goa and hatched a plot with some Jesuits to capture Bombay. The plot failed and—according to a periodical called *The Monthly Miscellany*—Cooke 'killed himself from mere vexation of spirit in his self-exile among the cowled brethren of the Order of Jesus'. In more literal terms, he died after falling from his horse.

The governors who followed Cooke did not fare much better. Nor did the soldiers, sailors and administrators. Bombay had acquired an evil reputation, one that compelled John Ovington, a chaplain with the East India Company, to remark a few years later that the island was 'nought but a charnel house' where two monsoons 'were the age of a man'.

Ovington's revulsion is understandable. He sailed to India on the *Benjamin* in 1691. Within four months of his arrival in Bombay, thirty-five of his shipmates had been buried. He perceived a city full of infection, wickedness and toads the size of small ducks; where English infants were particularly susceptible to the 'corruption of the air' and not 'one out of twenty of them live to any maturity'.

'Mendum's Point, a name more terrible to a sick Bombaian than the Inquisition to a heretick; a cormorant paunch never satisfied with the daily supplies it receives, but is still gaping for more tho' it hath swallowed more English flesh than the Bengal Tamarind Tree, Madras Guava Garden and the green hill at Bencala; yet still it hath room for those numbers twice told, and when digested, it will be as ravenous as ever,' wrote John Burnell, a soldier with the East India Company, in a letter to his father in 1711.

Burnell's letter is a chilling reminder of the realities of the 17th and 18th centuries, when shiploads of British soldiers and administrators died within months of landing in Bombay. So much so that when General John Gayer wrote to the Company demanding more soldiers, he remarked, 'The number sometime will not satisfy the craving of Mendham's Point above halfe one month.'

Burnell describes Mendham's Point as a cemetery with 140 large tombs. Some were topped with spires, others with pyramids, while still others—like one tomb shared by the Company's writers, or another, hastily prepared for an entire regiment—were cramped and basic.

Meanwhile, Charles II was broke and unwilling to send more men into Bombay's insatiable cemeteries; or more funds for the protection of swampy territory less than 18 square miles in area. Bombay was more trouble than it was worth and the English king readily signed it over to the East India Company for a farm rent of 10 pounds per annum.

Soon after the deed was finalized, Charles II and his advisors had reason to congratulate themselves. Bombay was attacked by the Sidi of Janjira, who not only captured the Sewri and Mazagaon Forts, but came dangerously close to Bombay Castle as well. Taunted and tormented by the Sidi, the Englishmen coughed up Rs 1.5 lakh as a sweetener for Aurangzeb. Only then were they allowed a semblance of peace.

While Bombay was being passed from hand to hand, however, what were the feelings of those who belonged to these lush, sleepy islands? Of the people who tilled the fields so prone to flooding? And of the fishermen whose hamlets dotted the islands? Bombay's original biographers—a motley crew of European travellers and administrators—viewed the local residents as irrelevant. So it's impossible to guess their sentiments during this colonial game of Passing the Parcel.

Equally frustrating is the fact that Colaba and Old Woman's Island are mere footnotes in the early history of Bombay. In 1634, a Portuguese official, Antonio Bocarro wrote in *Description of the Bar and Port of Mombaim* about the 'islet named Candil'. Forty years later, it pops up in British records as the Little Isle of Colio. Colaba and Old Woman's Island are often confused with each other or treated as a single entity.

What seems clear is that Colaba and Old Woman's

Island remained with the Portuguese even after the English claimed Bombay. Then, when the far-sighted Gerard Aungier took over as governor, he corrected this oversight. 'Colaba, or Old Woman's island as it was called for long, was taken possession of peaceably in 1674 after an arrangement made between Gerald Aungier and the Portuguese,' wrote Philip Anderson in *The English in Western India*. 'For many years it was only used to keep the company's antelopes and other beasts of delight. None of its land was appropriated to individuals, as from the first it was reserved to be a military cantonment.'

Why did the Portuguese—who were so reluctant to part with these islands—agree to this transfer? 'Probably,' wrote Jose Gerson da Cunha in *The Origin of Bombay*, 'because the barrenness of the rocky islet had shown them that it was not worth keeping any longer after the cession of its neighbouring island of Bombay to the British.'

Even after the British took control, Colaba remained barren and insignificant. John Burnell, a soldier and cartographer with the East India Company, estimated that the island's 'length is near two miles and in breadth hardly a quarter and half of dry ground, tho' on the west side is much mangrove and rocky land which stretcheth out near three quarters or a mile into the sea, visible at low water'. He mentioned a steep, rugged hill, a large grove of coconut trees and three kilns of chunam (lime) made from shells.

Somebody must have tended the kilns and climbed

those coconut trees. Still, there seems to have been little to disturb the antelopes and other beasts of delight other than a bunch of fleet-footed predators. In two newsy letters to his father, Burnell wrote about surveying the southernmost island in the early 1700s and attempting to shoot 'fifty or threescore jackalls' in the mangroves. 'They would fly like the wind and were always too nimble for me, for I could never shoot one,' he remarked.

In 1708, as meat was in short supply, the Company bred cattle in Colaba—which must have kept the 'fifty or threescore jackalls' very contented. After the meat crisis abated, the Company decided that the time had come to squeeze out some profit from this unpromising island and leased it out. In 1743, for example, a Mr Richard Broughton paid Rs 200 to renew his lease of the island for a period of twenty-one years. However, there are no records of the original lease or whether there were any tenants before him.

In 1734, a gun-powder mill with twenty-four pestles—to be powered either by buffaloes or by wind—was optimistically built on Old Woman's Island. The project flopped because the location was just too inconvenient. And so, Colaba was allowed to snooze once more.

The occasional mentions of Colaba from this period—including Lord Nelson's 1774 account of 'the lights of Old Woman's Island' from the Seahorse—conjure up a pristine place, sparsely populated and untouched by development. Barring two tall, white tombs, somewhere on the middle of the island.

One of the tombs belonged to Sir John Child, the luckless governor who had been compelled to strike a deal with the Sidi of Janjira. Distressed by his inability to evict the gutsy admiral and by vicious accusations of corruption, Sir John Child is supposed to have died of shame. He was buried in desolate Colaba, while a fleet of boats fired three volleys.

For over a century his tomb towered over the narrow island and greeted sea-weary sailors. 'References were also found to another large tower-like tomb known as the Jew's tomb or Moor's Sepulchre, situated probably where the Baptist Church now stands,' stated A.J. Nix-Seaman, who was the Archdeacon of Bombay in the 1930s and wrote a book called *The Afghan War Memorial Church and Historical Notes on Colaba*. 'Both tombs were white-washed and, being conspicuous by their height, were seen by sailors entering the harbour, and used by them as navigation guides in order to steer clear of the Sunken Rock.'

The Bombay Baptist Church that Nix-Seaman mentioned is a sturdy stone edifice that dispenses blessings near Colaba Post Office. It stands amidst a jumble of boxy buildings and grocery stores and it is disconcerting to think of a time when two white-washed tombs were all that rose from those rocks. No buildings called Shirin or Daulat, no buses or handcarts heaped with fruit. Just two silent sentinels, white against the empty sky.

Sir John Child's Tomb and the Moor's Sepulchre served

as both a welcome and a warning to the ships heading for Bombay. Colaba was notorious for its sneaky, submerged rocks and tragic shipwrecks, the most horrific of which involved two ships in 1840.

The *Lord William Bentinck* was sailing from London to Bombay, with about 200 passengers and troops on board. While *The Castlereagh* was heading to Bombay from Karrack with another 200 people on board. The monsoons had stormed into the city, and lashing wind and rain made it difficult for the *Lord William Bentinck* to enter the harbour. The ship waited at the mouth for a couple of days and then, during another attempt to reach the shore and safety, dashed against Prong's Reef, the deadly chain of rocks at the very tip of Colaba. The boat fell apart rapidly, and the gale was so violent that the rescue vessels and rafts were also dashed against the rocks. About hundred people died, but worse was to follow.

The *Lord Castlereagh* was also sailing to Bombay. Disoriented by the furious rain and waters, it mistook the lights of the *Lord William Bentinck* for the lights of the harbour—and crashed against the very same rocks.

'All along the beach, from Artha Bunder to the rocks at Malabar Point, could be seen evidences of the ruin that had been wrought during that fearful gale,' wrote F.W. Forrest in *Roughing It Out*, a book about the life of a British soldier. 'Broken masts, spars, barrels, bales, cabin furniture, ship's timbers, and hundreds of other articles, were strewn about in all directions; but by far the most appalling sight was the numerous dead bodies that were constantly being discovered amongst the clefts of rocks or on the sands, some fearfully lacerated, and some without a bruise. The life-boats and catamarans of the pilot service—the said catamarans are bamboo rafts which can live in any sea—were successful in rescuing many a poor fellow from a watery grave, but not a single female was saved. One young lady, daughter of a rich old Nawab, who was returning from England, where she had been sent to finish her education, offered to give her whole fortune, and marry the man that would save her. Several tried hard for the prize, but perished in the attempt. Many were twice-wrecked. The Bentinck went to pieces first, and several swam to the Castlereagh, and were hauled on board, but in a very short time she also went to pieces, and thus they were again cast upon the treacherous bosom of the angry waters.'

There are conflicting reports about how many people died in the waters of Colaba on that turbulent night. But Nix-Seaman mentioned that a single tomb in the Colaba Cemetery received '184 bodies, victims of the Castlereagh shipwreck'.

Over the centuries, other ships crashed into those vicious rocks and, till Prong's Lighthouse was built in 1875, dealing with the deceptive waters involved nifty navigation and arcane knowledge. For example, John Burnell recommended: 'To avoide the Sunken Rock or to know when you are northward or southward of it, bring Sir John Child's tomb to the westward of the seven trees and then you may be sure you are to the southward of it, these being the best and surest marks.'

Clearly, Colaba and its white tombs were critical when ships approached Bombay harbour. Once the passengers disembarked, however, the southernmost island held little interest. It was no more than a health resort for the military and a salubrious spot where local merchants sent their sick daughters.

In 1769, however, Colonel Pemble wrote an impassioned letter to the government, asking that troops be allowed to stay in Colaba all year round. 'The great benefit the Europeans have derived from the short time they have encamped there is obvious in every point. Drunkenness, that bane to discipline, appears already in a manner abolished and the health of the men consequently better preserved. The salubrity of the situation is likewise a very favourable circumstance,' he stated, adding—rather mystifyingly—that in Colaba the troops amused themselves in a 'rational and manly manner instead of sinking into every kind of debauchery'.

The letter achieved its purpose and Colaba soon acquired barracks and villas to accommodate the men of the military and save them from debauchery. A few wily officers took advantage of the flurry of construction to build private houses. There were, for example, the two houses built by one General Waddington that caused quite a brouhaha.

In 1793, the government threatened to take over the General's houses and use them as military quarters. General Waddington protested, lobbied and managed to lease the land on which his houses were built. Eventually this property passed on to his daughter, Mrs Hough—whose name pops up in books about Bombay for an unusual reason. Jose Gerson da Cunha wrote that this grand old lady's garden in Colaba 'had a mango tree which used to fruit twice yearly, at Christmas, as well as in the usual season of mangoes, in May'.

Mrs Hough's property was sold to the BB and CI Railway. You've probably guessed what's coming next. This was the land that was used for Colaba Station.

Old Colaba Station, 1896–1930. *Source: Wikimedia Commons.*

This is the land I see whenever I stand at my window.

Once more I rush to the window to gaze at the blocky red and white buildings of Badhwar Park visible behind the venerable banyan tree. Before this mundane crop of buildings came along, there was Colaba Station with its shingled roof and puffing trains. And before that, a garden with a mango tree that fruited twice a year—and a house that, in true Mumbai tradition, was built on encroached land.

Old Mrs Hough—who danced with Arthur Wellesley, Duke of Wellington, during his visit to Bombay—has gone. So has her controversial house. But could the diligent mango tree still be standing in Badhwar Park? Or in Cusrow Baug, which replaced the old railway goods yard?

Mango trees have a lifespan of about 300 years. Could the tree have escaped the axe when the garden was cleared for trains, yards and buildings? For that matter, could the broad and nurturing banyan outside my window have been a part of Mrs Hough's famed estate? Or could the sturdy stone wall—today covered with red-blue-pink graffiti, a beloved backdrop of selfie-takers, YouTubers and TikTokers—have once contained the estate of the ancient Mrs Hough?

It's a gooseflesh-creating thought. Suddenly, the past feels close enough to touch.

(Colaba Lesson for Life—The dragonflies whirring past the stone wall and banyan tree are amazing. They are part of a massive, annual, inter-generational migration from India to East Africa—the longest insect migration that we know about.)

5. A Creek too Far

'I decided that my first stop, therefore, should be a British cemetery marked on a map in my recent guidebook. I took a taxi down to Moscow Lane, at the very tip of Colaba Causeway and began walking past cannons and Connaught Barracks, past an "officer's mess" and "Single Officers Accommodation" bungalows—all the way down to an abandoned lighthouse. Not seeing any sign of English tombstones, I turned into the Indian Institute of Geomagnetism and asked a passing geomagnetist where they might be. He asked a passing non-geomagnetist, found out that the cemetery was now a high school, and said rather gallantly, "Good bye my dear" as I trooped off. Behind us, in the back of the old army school, a man was standing solemnly in khaki shorts, in the middle of a huge patch of empty grass, practicing "Reveille" on his trumpet.'

—Pico Iyer in his essay,
'Bombay: Hobson-Jobson on the Streets'

It was in the early 19th century that the antelopes and jackals of Colaba were seriously disturbed for the first time. The Colaba Cemetery was built in 1816 and served as a final resting place for soldiers and victims of shipwrecks. Then the Colaba Observatory and Lunatic Asylum were built in 1826—close to where the US Club stands today.

The Colaba Lunatic Asylum was a doleful place where patients were beaten, compelled to sleep on sacks of straw and forced to have cold showers. 'The tiny island of Colaba, with its ideal view of the Bombay harbour and the surrounding countryside was an island of paradoxes,' wrote Sarah Ann Pinto in *Lunatic Asylums in Colonial Bombay: Shackled Bodies, Unchained Minds*. 'A noisy village covered a part of the island, while two burial grounds (English and Muslim) covered the other. On its western shore lay the Colaba Lunatic Asylum...The pleasant views from the Colaba Lunatic Asylum, however, contrasted with the sounds emanating from it. John Murray, in his account of Bombay city, observed that the English cemetery, "though tolerably well kept, was rendered dismal by having a lunatic asylum adjoining it...and walking about to examine the tombs the cries of the unhappy inmates are constantly heard".'

Those tombs of shipwreck victims and that lunatic asylum now exist only in brittle, yellowing books. But whenever I visit US Club, I stand at lands' end and look towards Prong's Lighthouse, listening for the cries of the terrified souls on board *The Castlereagh* on that stormy, ill-fated night. And of the equally unfortunate souls incarcerated in that unhappy asylum. On certain wind-whipped days, I'm almost convinced that I hear them. And all the jesting golfers and swinging children, sunshine and sea-light cannot obliterate the sudden darkness.

Even amidst death and madness, however, the light of religion was determined to shine upon Colaba. Christianity had begun to assert itself in Bombay, and as Archdeacon Nix-Seaman remarked, Colaba was 'stirred by the same awakening'. First came the little Catholic chapel near Colaba Post Office that was later used by the Portuguese Government to house officials on their way to Goa. Then came the RC Military Church, best known because it is the southernmost bus terminus in the city.

Not to be outdone, the Church of England began to fuss about the spiritual well-being of its flock in remote Colaba. The beleaguered authorities agreed to contribute Rs 28,151—not a paisa more, not a paisa less!—towards a Protestant chapel, but this was considered inadequate. After much haggling, a temporary church with a thatched roof and without chairs was cobbled together—scandalizing the Bishop of Calcutta who, in 1835, refused to 'consecrate so rickety a building'. Eventually it was replaced by the serene Afghan Church in 1858.

Despite the spurt of activity, the Lunatic Asylum and Bring-Your-Own-Chairs church were not exactly a draw for house hunters. Especially after Colaba's reputation as the healthiest spot in Bombay was overturned by a deadly malaria epidemic that had the authorities grousing that it was the 'most unhealthy station for European troops'.

The 1826 census found that the population of Colaba was a measly 2,578—less than 2 per cent of the 1.3 lakh inhabitants of Bombay. To make matters worse, Colaba was depicted as a veritable den of menacing criminals, dangerous animals and single-bite-and-it's-all-over snakes. Jackals slunk around the Colaba Observatory and boldly wandered into bedrooms. Snakes were regular worshippers at the Afghan Church, coiling around its pillars and hiding in the organ. While Mr Forjett—possibly the same gentleman who gave his name to Forjett Street—even shot a tiger near Backbay.

In 1828, a huge shark was spotted near some bathers. Two decades later, a finback whale was driven to shore. *The Gentlemen's Gazette* reported that, 'All along the road from the Fort to Colaba was a perfect fair. The stench was felt from the town side of the causeway from where it lay at the back of Colaba church. Jawbones taken away.'

More troublesome than the snakes and smelly sharks even, were the 'Mahratta gallivants'. In *Glimpses of Bombay and Western India*, James Douglas—who was once the sheriff of Bombay—recounted that 'On October 14, 1798, a stranger happening to be in the Colaba Light House, observed that a peaceable dinghy was being attacked off the harbor by five Mahratta gallivants, throwing in shots, burning her to the water's edge, when she blew up leaving her crew the choice of the flames or a watery grave.'

So pesky was the Bandar Gang that prowled around the Backbay, that a floating police force was established to tackle it. Meanwhile, the terrestrial police force had its own set of villains and woes. In 1827, for example, one Mrs Sparrow was returning from church in her carriage when she was attacked by a mounted Armenian who shot away her coachman's ear. 'About that time, a gentleman was deterred from buying the "Wilderness" because it was so remote, and exposed to the attack of robbers,' remarked Douglas.

Clearly, Colaba—with its mosquito-riddled mangroves and criminal-infested bays—was an undesirable spot in the early 1800s. So, it's startling to read Henry Moses' enthusiastic description in 1848, just twenty-one years after Mrs Sparrow's poor coachman lost his ear.

'It is considered a healthy place of residence, being freely exposed to the sea breeze; and its beauty is greatly enhanced by the charming view which it commands on all sides,' wrote Moses in *Sketches of India: With Notes on the Seasons, Scenery and Society of Bombay*. 'In consequence of these advantages it is crowded with English, Parsee and Portuguese bungalows; which are all detached residences, surrounded by luxuriant gardens, redolent of sweet flowers...The boundary hedges are enriched by a charming creeping plant which bears a scarlet and sometimes a rich mazarine-blue pea flower. When in full bloom the plants add greatly to the beauty of the gardens.'

What happened in two short decades that so completely transformed Colaba? The answer is simple: Colaba Causeway.

The dictionary defines a 'causeway' as 'a raised road or track across low or wet ground'. Colaba Causeway was exactly that. The elevated road had been proposed for decades, but it was only in 1838 that Old Woman's Island and Colaba Island were connected to Bombay by a simple strip of stone, mud and timber. The impact was immediate and the price of land in Colaba shot up by 500 per cent in a single decade.

Colaba Causeway construction using timber, viewed from Colaba island, 1826. Lithograph by Jose M. Gonsalves (1826–1842). *Source: Wikimedia Commons.*

Till 1838, travelling from Bombay to Colaba had involved crossing a smelly creek. At low tide this could be traversed 'dry shod'. But at high tide the journey could only be made by boat. This was why Mrs Postans, that most observant of travel writers, dismissed the southernmost island as a pretty but dull spot, favoured only by those who preferred 'quiet to the gaieties of the sister land'.

'Many have been the luckless wights who, returning from a festive meeting, heedless of Neptune's certain visit, have found the curling waves beating over their homeward path, compelling them again to seek the banquet hall deserted and beg a shakedown at the quarters of their host,' she wrote. 'The more impetuous have sought to swim their horses across the dangerous pass and lives have been lost in the attempt. This inconvenience so severely felt led at length to the erection of a solid and handsome vallade with a footpath protecting the elevated and level road.'

Reading Mrs Postan's words, a piece of a historic puzzle falls into place.

Whenever you are next near Regal Cinema, take a good look at the Office of the Director General of Police which, when it was first built, was the Royal Alfred Sailor's Home. The pediment of this chunky building features Neptune brandishing a trident and frolicking with sea horses. Suddenly his presence at this busy, traffic-clogged intersection makes sense. Not so long ago, all this was a creek. The God of the Sea is merely keeping tabs on his former territory.

Just as Regal Cinema is merely continuing the tradition of drama that this spot witnessed. Take, for example, the tale that Henry Moses relates in the purplest prose:

> A melancholy and romantic story is still told of Colabah...A young girl of the Mohammedan faith was on her road to pay a visit to some natives who resided in Colabah; and having arrived in her bullock gharry just when the tide was rising in this place, she thought, that as the water was not deep, she might cross without danger, and ordered her syce or driver to order the timid bullocks across the stream. He did so; but before they had proceeded many yards, the animals became restive and obstinate and refused to go one way or another; the wheels became entangled among the rough stones; the gharry was upset and the poor girl being thrown into the rapidly increasing current, was swept out into Back Bay. This scene was witnessed most fortunately from the Colabah side, by an Englishman, who had upto this moment been a passive spectator. In an instant his coat was off and he was breasting the foaming tide after the drowning girl; whom, at the risk of his own life he succeeded in bringing safely to the shore. He accompanied her home to Bombay where he received the thanks and benedictions of her parents. Strange to say, though not more strange than true, an attachment sprang up between the young Englishman and the Hindoo lady whom he had rescued from a watery grave; and many were said to be the private meetings that took place between the two lovers—unknown, of course, to the unsuspecting parents.

> At length the Englishman, though he knew that his religion would be an impenetrable objection, determined to solicit from her father, the Mohammedan girl's hand in marriage. He did so, and the haughty man of high caste at once indignantly spurned his proposals. He acknowledged that he loved the fair Englishman but never could be one of his people; so he bade him depart in peace. The sequel was very sad. The Hindoo maiden disappeared. Rumours were current, in Bombay, that she had been privately murdered by her enraged relatives…

The Englishman died of a broken heart. The family left the island.

What happened to the bullocks and the syce—stuck in the foaming, rising waters—is not known. Nor is it known whether the unfortunate maiden was 'Mohammedan' or 'Hindoo'. But this story is an apt precursor to the Bollywood blockbusters that would one day be screened at that very spot—on the big screen of Regal Cinema.

(Colaba Lesson for Life—Through much of the 19th century, there were strict restrictions on the use of iron and electricity in Colaba. This was to ensure that the magnetic readings of the Colaba Observatory were not vitiated. In fact, electric trams were given permission to run only after a replacement observatory was built in Alibag and tested in 1907. Alibag was deprived of electricity all the way till 1954. It's unnerving to think of what Colaba might have been today if the Observatory had not been moved.)

6. An Island No More

'We used to live in Churchgate but we moved into a bungalow in Cuffe Parade around 1949-50. Our house was just about 20 feet from the promenade. It was an exceptionally beautiful area, and the most expensive. Where World Trade Centre now stands was a swamp where crows used to breed. Where Badhwar Park now stands was just stones and grass and railway tracks. In fact, the entire area up to Marine Drive was just sea and stones. At that point Bombay was one of the most beautiful cities in the world.'

—Munis Varawalla, ninety-three, recalls a very different Colaba, with soldiers training on the roads, open spaces and kacha roads

As long as it was separated from the rest of Bombay by an unruly creek, Colaba retained its turtles, its mangroves and its reputation as the backwaters of Bombay. This distinct identity existed not just in the minds of harassed commuters but in the reckoning of the administration. Be it the 'Rules for the removal of balconies projecting over or encroaching upon any public thoroughfare in the islands of Bombay and Colaba–1839' or the 'Bathing in Public Tanks prohibited in Bombay and Colaba–1842', there's plenty of evidence that Colaba was an independent entity.

With the changes in geography, however, came other changes. The famous turtles disappeared—which was sad. The name Old Woman's Island disappeared too—which was not.

Soon, it was difficult to remember that once this had been a detached clump of fine-grained diorite rocks, besieged by swamps, swirling tides and jackal-infested mangroves. That once this was the domain of the Kolis till, as Salman Rushdie wrote in his novel *Midnight's Children*, 'A Fort and afterwards a city took their land; pile-drivers stole (tetrapods would steal) pieces of their sea. But there are still Arab dhows, every evening, spreading their sails against the sunset...'

Today, in an age when sea links and coastal roads are so nonchalantly built, a mere causeway across a creek would barely merit six inches of newsprint. But Colaba Causeway had an unimaginable impact on the Bombay of the 19th century. Suddenly, it was possible to toddle across to Colaba without checking on tides or becoming the protagonist of a tragic love story.

A vintage postcard depicting the Colaba reclamation.
Source: Wikimedia Commons.

Canny businessmen and traders—as fleet-footed and opportunistic as the jackals they replaced—were the first to spot the open spaces and to move in for the kill. The combination of cheap real estate and proximity to the docks made Colaba an irresistible proposition. Not for their fancy bungalows, which were located at Mazagaon and Malabar Hill, Byculla and Parel, but for warehouses and workshops.

In 1863, Govind Narayan, a prolific Marathi writer and magazine editor, published a biography of Bombay, called *Mumbaiche Varnan* (A Description of Bombay). In it, he described a Colaba that is drab and unfamiliar. Just two decades after the Causeway was built, Colaba had become a dumping ground for all manner of unlovely things—heaps of coal, piles of wood, noisy factories. Not to forget a lunatic asylum and a dark house in which disobedient military men were punished in terrible ways:

> It has already been mentioned that Colaba was a desolate place. Considering the place to be totally useless, the government auctioned it off at a cheap price some years back. The land that was sold off at five hundred rupees now yields a monthly produce of a thousand rupees.
>
> The creek towards the north-west of Colaba has been filled up and is now used to store bales of cotton and piles of wood. A few warehouses have been built here and it is felt that in a while bungalows will come up in this place. Colaba has been divided into three imaginary parts—Little Colaba, from Arthur Bunder Road to the Gun Carriage; Middle Colaba reaching up to the Kabul Church, and further ahead is Upper Colaba, extending up to the very tip of the land or the Dandi.
>
> At the head of Little Colaba is Arthur Bunder; on the jetty stands the Grant Building; behind it are two very large mills. There are many warehouses for storing cotton. Sir Jamsetjee Jijibhoy and his partners have built a wharf for unloading their goods at an expense of around one and a half lakh rupees. They have a large factory here in which are installed eight machines that run on steam. Many other businesses have their offices here.
>
> The houses of the white regiments, the Hospital and the Portuguese and English churches are situated in Middle Colaba. In the year 1848, a church was built in memory

> of the soldiers who fell in the battle at Kabul and is called the Kabul Church. It is estimated that 80,000 rupees were spent on this church. Further ahead are the military training grounds then the Kolse Bunder, many houses and a small market. Near the market is a building known as Kanji House, a dark mansion in which offending soldiers are punished.
>
> Moving on to Upper Colaba, one first passes the bungalows of the sahibs and then the Observatory, which should certainly be visited by all students…Further ahead is the tip of Colaba. There is a madhouse to confine lunatics. At the very end is a small fortress on which two cannons have been mounted. There is an English cemetery at the far end of the fortress where many English tombs have been built.

Colaba seemed set to become a Dickensian hellhole. A place of smoking chimneys and soot, clattering machines and factories leaking virulent green slime. How then did it escape becoming the industrial armpit of Bombay? How did it manage to metamorphose into an area of peach melba and expensive dressmakers, purple-sashed archbishops and lavender-haired matrons? Thanks, largely, to the winds of change blowing in from distant shores

In 1857, all of India was rocked by the revolt against the British Raj. Compared to north India, Bombay stayed peaceful. Despite whispers of some 'Gunga Pursad business' (dangafasaad or riots, to you and me) it was business as usual—barring one night of rumours when the Europeans of Colaba retreated onto the ships in the harbour to escape murderous hordes. Hordes that never came, had never existed even.

In 1858, the East India Company was abolished and Bombay—like the rest of India—passed into the hands of the British government. Meanwhile, Bombay was witnessing a growth spurt. Creeks were filled, causeways extended and reclamation companies formed: Mazagaon Land and Reclamation Company; Backbay Reclamation Company; Colaba Land and Reclamation Company; Frere Land and Reclamation Company. 'In the sixties, owing to the increased commercial activity the population of Bombay was daily increasing in number,' wrote Rekha Ranade in *Sir Bartle Frere and His Times: A Study of His Bombay Years, 1862-1867*. 'The value of the land had been trebled and quadrupled in Bombay, and as the available space within the island was very little "every additional foot tacked on seemed likely to be worth its weight in gold".'

Colaba was no exception. A series of schemes transformed Colaba from a scrawny teenager into an ample matron. For in those heady years in the 1860s—well before its environmental impact was understood—reclamation was the solution to every problem.

Need somewhere to store cotton near the docks of Apollo Bunder? No problem. Launch the Apollo Bay Reclamation. And if you're at it anyway, might as well create land for a middle-class residential precinct, a magnificent hotel and a Europeans-only club as well.

Need to lay railway tracks from Grant Road to Colaba? Jump into the ambitious Backbay Reclamation Scheme of the 1860s and conjure up a swathe of land from Malabar Hill to the tip of Colaba.

The Bombay of the 1860s was marked by a sense of invincibility. In America, a war was being fought. Elsewhere, a canal was being built that connected the Red Sea and the Mediterranean Sea. These events unleashed forces that whooshed across the globe and propelled Colaba towards its destiny.

The American civil war was fought between 1861 and 1865. In an attempt to hold the world to ransom, the American South embargoed cotton exports and burnt 2.5 million bales. Later, the North imposed its own blockades. The 'cotton famine' starved the rapacious English mills, which needed a steady diet of raw materials. Frantic, they turned to the humble, short-staple cotton of India. Prices skyrocketed and the local cotton trade went bazooka.

The hunger for cotton was so great that people ripped apart their mattresses and pillows to sell the 'white gold'. 'King Cotton was the great deity at whose shrine…the merchant and the banker, the rich and the poor, high and low, the master and servant all paid,' wrote Dinshaw Vacha, one of the founder members of the Indian National Congress, about those frenzied times.

A bulk of the cotton travelled from the loamy fields of India to the dark mills of England via Bombay. It was here that the cotton was traded, loaded onto ships and sent on to the mill towns of northern England. Little wonder, then, that during the American civil war, the city became richer by a staggering 80 million pounds.

Of this newfound wealth, about 6 million pounds went into extending Bombay into the sea. This resulted in speculation, wild schemes, scams—and a few brave ideas that eventually transformed Bombay into a livable city with electric lights, sanitation and civic sensibilities.

The distant war ended in 1865 and the inevitable crash occurred. Fortunes and companies crumbled, jobs disappeared, and ambitions collapsed. Still, as Edwardes pointed out, it was soon apparent that Bombay had 'suffered no permanent injury from the wild excesses of these five years'.

This was largely due to another stroke of luck. In 1869 the Suez Canal opened, reducing the sea voyage between Bombay and London by a whopping three-quarters. The Bombay port speedily overtook the Calcutta port in volume of trade. And more than any other locality, Colaba had reason to rejoice.

Today, the name Cotton Green is associated with a distinctly not-green station on the Harbour Line. So, it comes as a shock that this higgle-piggle of houses, shanties and workshops was once an actual Cotton Green where

The cotton market, at Bombay, an engraving from 'India and its Native Princes' by Louis Rousselet, 1878. *Source: Wikimedia Commons.*

bales of cotton were heaped, bought and sold. It comes as an even greater shock that the earlier Cotton Green—the one that witnessed those heady, money-minting years—was located in Colaba.

The city's very first Cotton Green was at Elphinstone Circle—the garden ringed by handsome buildings, designer stores and trendy coffee shops that we now know as Horniman Circle. In the early 1800s, this was the heart of busy, crowded Fort and the confusion of cotton bales and impervious traders contributed to the existing chaos. In 1844, after numerous complaints and aggrieved 'Letters to the Editor', the Cotton Green was shifted to its new home: the no longer remote, no longer island of Colaba.

Why Colaba? As far as the British were concerned, cotton came to Bombay only so that it could be sent to the insatiable mills of Lancashire, Yorkshire and Manchester. 'Bombay's cotton industry was then in an embryonic state,' wrote M.I. Dantwala in *A Hundred Years of Indian Cotton.* 'In the forties, if cotton came to Bombay it was mainly for export. Colaba, with its big open spaces and proximity to the harbor of those days, was best suited as a cotton market.'

The Cotton Green squatted on 1.5 square miles on either side of the Causeway. It occupied the large yard where, today, BEST buses go to bed every night. But it also continued southwards towards Colaba Market. Which means that a hundred years ago, my daily walk from

Fort Convent to the irregular plot of land where Batra House would one day be built would have been utterly unrecognizable. Instead of Art Deco buildings and vendors of flipflops, I would have walked past a sun-baked space scattered with warehouses and bales of cotton; agog with businessmen and brokers.

Nothing familiar, besides the chink-chink of the taal emanating from the Bhid Bhanjan Mahadev Mandir. And the bulk of Grant's Building—which in those days was envisaged as a major mercantile centre. (Grant's Building still stands on Arthur Bunder Road, but it never did fulfil its Bandra-Kurla-Complex-type destiny. Chiku Advani, who has lived across from the building for over seventy years, recalls that it was later used as a dormitory for sailors—and for their convenience, housed a couple of brothels as well. Today the historic building is a haphazard mix of art galleries, attar shops, shoe boutiques and hobby classes for children.)

The Cotton Green brought cotton bales, mills and bullock carts to Colaba. It also brought tourists. And the numerous accounts of travellers—although prejudiced, even downright racist—offer a fleeting glimpse into a forgotten past. 'The Cotton Exchange is the general meeting place between buyers and sellers, business beginning soon after midday,' wrote James Maclean in his 1875 guidebook to Bombay. 'The European merchant, through his dalal or broker, arranges the price and terms of purchase—a matter which owing to the native love of bargaining is a much more lengthy process than it would be in England.'

In his spiteful but newsy *Letters from Bombay*, written in 1884, D. Aubrey rattled on about summer afternoons rife with wheeling and dealing:

> At about 3 pm the Cotton Exchange near the Cathedral becomes densely crowded. Here, in the centre of public thoroughfare, broker and merchants transact their affairs. Wealthy bania merchants and Parsi brokers slip from their own carriages into each others' vehicles, sit for a while in the conveyance till the bargain is struck or refused. The poorer trader discusses his business under a coloured umbrella, chattering over files of sordid papers and sordid books, to squeeze out a pice or to secure an upcountry order. English merchants also drive down in the shigram or brougham and their agility in leaping from one vehicle to another favourably contrasts with the sloth and awkwardness of the native when exchanging carriages. Difficult is it for the occidentals to counteract the cunning of the native brokers who play into each other's hands to baffle the European and to commit every deed of craftiness that can be practiced within and without the pale of law. The degree of calmness they preserve throughout their bargains defeats all the arts that can be opposed to it.

A few years later, in 1890, W.S. Caine provided a bedazzled description in *Picturesque India: A Handbook for European Travellers*:

> Bombay, after New Orleans, is the greatest cotton port in the world, and a visit should be paid to the Cotton Green about noon, at which time 'high change' sets in at a yard opposite to the Colaba terminus of the tramway, Any open market in India is sure to be a striking picture of native life, brightened with an endless variety of costume and kaleidoscopic colour. The cotton market of Bombay is no exception. Four million cwts. are exported from Bombay in the year, and over two millions more are consumed in the 82 mills in the Bombay Presidency, the bulk of which are in the city; the value of all this cotton is about twelve million sterling.

Which sounds most impressive till you think about the nitty-gritties. Even in 1851, well before the boom, Mr Chapman, the founder-manager of the Great Indian Peninsula Railway Company noted that the '18,000 tonnes of cotton, the quantity now brought down to Bombay, require 1,80,000 bullocks to carry them…'

In this situation it made perfect sense to extend the railway all the way to the Cotton Green. Colaba Station opened in 1872 and the rest of Bombay heaved a sigh of relief. Colaba, though, could not join in with its hosannas. For after the bales of cotton chugged into the station, they were transported by bullock cart to the Cotton Green. There they were subjected to bargaining and scrutiny, after which they were dispatched to the docks—which involved another procession of plodding, potty-depositing carts.

Those tales of bullock-cart jams serve a purpose. They remind us not to wish too hard for the good old days. At least, not until we've done our research.

I've done my research, though, and know many things I didn't before: that before it became a shopping paradise and tourist hangout, Colaba Causeway was thick with slow-moving bullock carts and quadruple-parked carriages of cotton traders.

That it was fitting that as a schoolgirl I should have borrowed *Gone with the Wind* from a library run out of an old tin trunk on Colaba Causeway. This was where the old Cotton Green had once stood, and where the city had witnessed the cotton frenzy unleashed by the American civil war. The forces that transformed Scarlett O'Hara's world were the same forces that transformed Colaba.

That before it became a quiet lane shaded by copper pods and mango trees, my corner of Colaba was awhirl with scheming and dealing. That cotton tycoons like Premchand Roychand—the man behind the first financial crash in the city—could well have wheedled, whispered and struck bargains beneath the wise, wide banyan tree. Almost exactly where I am sitting now at an oval desk, next to a window that looks onto Badhwar Park/Colaba Station/Mrs Hough's Garden/a patch of wilderness sloping into a creek.

That Roychand and his cronies probably walked down to the Bhid Bhanjan Mahadev Mandir to offer their thanksgiving—every time I pass the peach-coloured mandir on Colaba Causeway I gaze at it with awe. As the temple at the heart of the city's cotton boom, it must have been privy to the juiciest secrets in town.

That the infamous cotton fires of the early 1900s must have raged just minutes from here, spreading heat, smoke and devastation. Those blazes destroyed lakhs worth of cotton and, even today, remain a puzzle. Were the fires part of an insurance scam? Or a genuine case of spontaneous combustion? S.M. Edwardes who besides being a prolific writer was also the city's police chief, maintained that, 'The huge cotton fires which have from time to time caused a scandal at the old Colaba Cotton Green in Bombay were undoubtedly fraudulent in origin, despite attempts to ascribe their outbreak to spontaneous combustion. Often it was found that the cotton had been fraudulently mixed or that it had been insured for more than it had been worth...'

That these fires were spectacles that made their way into police reports and paperback romances. In her 1917 novel called *Jan and Her Job*, Lizzie Allen Harker describes the inferno:

> There had been a great fire in the cotton green towards Colaba. It had blazed all night and in spite of the efforts of the Bombay firemen and their engines was still blazing at six o'clock the following evening.
>
> Peter took Jan out in his car to see it. There was an immense crowd so they left the car on its outskirts and plunged into the throng on foot. On either side of the

road were tall, flimsy houses with a wooden staircase outside; those curious tenements so characteristic of the poorer parts of Bombay, and in such marked contrast to the Fort, the European quarter of the town. They were occupied chiefly by Eurasians and very poor Europeans. That the road was a sea of mud varied by quite deep pools of water, seemed the only possible reason why the houses were not also burning.

Jan splashed bravely through the mud, interested and excited by the people and the leaping flames so dangerously near. It was growing dusk; the air was full of the acrid smell of burnt cotton; and the red glow from the sky was reflected on the grave brown faces watching the fire.

Any crowd in Bombay is always extremely varied and Jan almost forgot her anxieties in her enjoyment of the picturesque scene.

'I don't think the people ought to be allowed to throng on the top of that staircase,' Peter said suddenly. 'They aren't built to hold a number at once; there'll be an accident,' and he left her side for a moment to speak to an inspector of police.

Jan looked up at a tall house on her left where sightseers were collecting on the staircase to get a better view. Every window was crowded with gazers. All but one. From one, quite at the top, a solitary watcher looked out.

There was a sudden shout from the crowd below, a redder glow as more piled cotton fell into the general furnace and blazed up, and in that moment Jan saw that the solitary watcher was Hugo Tancred, and that he recognized her. She gave a little gasp of horror…

I now know that Mahatma Gandhi came here during a moderately successful Fund Collection Drive on 4 July 1921. *The History of the Freedom Movement, Volume 9* informs us that 'Mathurdas Vasanji Khimji gave a purse of approximately Rs 1,54,000 on behalf of the Colaba Cotton Merchants. A motorcar valued at about Rs 12,000 was presented by one Durgadulji and put up for auction: but the highest bid was only Rs 6,500. It was therefore knocked down and is at present one of the assets of the Swaraj Fund. Two bales of cotton were also put up for auction; the one on which Gandhi was sitting went at Rs 6,100; the other not so pleasantly favoured fetched Rs 2,500.'

That, if I were to go back to my corner of Colaba even 100 years ago, I wouldn't recognize it at all.

That finally Colaba's time had come.

(Lesson for Life on a Colaba T-shirt—Entry late hogi, par great hogi.)

7. Dreaming in Stone

'Colaba is one place where you can still feel the past. The old names like Duxbury Lane, Napier Road and Magdalene House tell us about the history of the area. Accommodation Road got its name from the Police Accommodation Scheme. The pillars on the buildings of Colaba Causeway came from England by ship and have stood the test of time. If you look carefully, you can read names of the companies that manufactured them. Olympia Coffee House and Stores was called that because it was exactly that—a shop and Irani café. The restaurant was across the road. I remember the owner was murdered in 1948. The guesthouse at Buckley Court was run by Armenians and we police knew, of course, that it was a love nest. There was a Japanese hotel run in Sentinel House till 1937.'

—Deepak Rao, former police officer and ardent history buff, who has special affection for the lanes and buildings of Colaba

There was a time, not so long ago, when nobody ventured into Colaba. Then, all of a sudden, everybody seemed to be heading this way.

For visitors who stepped out of a train at Colaba Station or off a ship at Apollo Bunder, Colaba was an easy destination. Like other areas that develop around ports worldwide, it was a beguiling mix of languages and currencies, Italian restaurants, Japanese hotels, Arab traders and Armenian emigres. It was an area that was rough and charming, gritty and wide-eyed, all at the same time. A neighbourhood that absorbed fortune-hunters and holiday-makers, millionaires and gamblers, the flotsam and jetsam.

It was the obvious home for women with dubious reputations and Mata Hari accents. For solitary Englishmen who decided to stay on in Bombay even when sense and convention dictated that they go back home. For poets, artists and displaced Jewish families. Gradually this would become my grandmother's Bombay, Aurora Zogoiby's Bombay, Baumgartner's Bombay. And, of course, my Bombay.

That, though, was in the future.

In the middle of the 19th century, the causeway was still being widened. Pieces of land were being fitted jigsaw-like along the shoreline. Buildings and landmarks were being translated from imagination into stone. There was still air and water where today there is cement and certainty.

The arrival of trains and trams in the 1870s dispelled the

sea-lapped silence and hick-town reputation. 'The horse-drawn tram and the railway line brought a certain romance of travel to the area,' wrote railway expert Rajendra Aklekar in his book *Halt Station India*. 'And as crowds increased, the railways took up a project to convert the small Colaba station into a major terminus. A station building came up in 1893.'

Not all of Colaba was in a hurry to grow up, however. Upper Colaba and parts of Middle Colaba clung to their sleepy ways. The area was then—as it is now—reserved for the military and remained suspended in the amber of antiquated rules and conventions.

In *Just Because*, an otherwise dreary novel published in 1915, Margaret Peterson described the hermetically sealed world of the military station, with its scheming memsahibs, capable bearers and indiscreet dalliance. The rest of the city is devastated by plague, suspicion and funerals, but here are tea parties and summer frocks as usual:

> A row of servants were drawn up in a line to welcome the dog-cart as it turned in the garden gates. In command of the party was a fat stately gentleman arrayed in spotless linen who announced himself as the cook and took it upon himself to introduce the rest of the staff. There was the table boy, the hamal—the knife and lamp cleaner, two punkah coolies, two malis, three syces, the sweeper and last but not the least, 'a most honest woman', as the cook described her, who had been introduced by the ayah

next door and who craved the honour of attending to the revered new mistress of Drummond Sahib's bungalow.

Even in this realm of knife-cleaners, towering trees and low-slung military bungalows, however, change was afoot. The Colaba Agiary was built in 1836. It was announced with a letter dated March 9, entreating 'the European and Native Gentlemen of Our Presidency' to permit their 'Parsee clerks and servants to attend an important Ceremony at the church newly erected by Jeejeebhoy Dadabhoy at Colaba on Tuesday the 15th March Instant. A compliance with the above request will Confer a great favour.'

Whether the European and Native Gentlemen complied is not known. What is known, however, is that the location of the fire temple was most inconvenient. In the early years, it could only be accessed by boat and even when roads were laid, Parsi women avoided wearing jewellery when they ventured into those badlands. So it's ironic that today the Colaba Agiary is booked years in advance for fairytale weddings and navjotes—and sees the most eye-popping display of diamonds, rubies and emeralds imaginable.

Just around the corner, the lovely Afghan Church started to rise in 1847, in memory of the dreadful massacre that was the first Anglo-Afghan War. By 1858, its honey-hued spire had risen into the salty, clammy air. The names of the slain officers had been written on its walls.

The Great Game was at its heights when the British—paranoid that Russia would try to annexe India—marched

Afghan Church, Interior view, c.1880–90.
Source: Wikimedia Commons.

into Afghanistan in 1838. After four years of guerrilla warfare and skirmishes, interference and politics, they agreed to depart if their 4,500 soldiers and 12,000 camp followers were given safe passage. The unwieldly procession was making its way through the treacherous, snowbound Hindu Kush and was traversing a pass, five miles long and 'so narrow and so shut in on either side that the wintry sun rarely penetrates its gloomy recesses', when the Ghilzai tribals attacked. The outcome was a bloodbath that left thousands dead. Those who survived—largely women and children—were taken prisoners. Of those 16,500 individuals, only one officer and a handful of sepoys managed to escape to India.

This haunting story reverberates in my head when I visit Afghan Church one mundane Thursday morning. Standing in the middle of an overgrown garden, the church seems far away from the BEST buses and schoolchildren rattling away outside. And, stepping into its eerie hush, it's easy to rewind to a time when the tragedy was still raw. When snakes and jackals were a part of the congregation. When the English officers worshipped with their rifles at hand, positioned in slots in the pews—in case of another 1857-type situation. And when the British imagined that they would be worshipping in this church for centuries to come.

Prong's Lighthouse—at the tip of deadly Prong's Reef—is equally evocative. The red and white lighthouse was built in 1875 and is the best-known of the three sentinels that flash their warning lights by the Mumbai harbour. Looking at it from the shore, it's difficult to guess that this lighthouse has eight rooms, including living quarters for six people. And that once it was equipped with a cannon to repel pirates.

Prong's Lighthouse was one of the numerous projects undertaken to transform Bombay into a safe and convenient port. After the Suez Canal opened and more ships chose to sail to Bombay, it became obvious that the city's docking facilities were woefully inadequate. Albert-Abdullah Sassoon—the son of David Sassoon, the Baghdadi Jewish merchant, who had made Bombay his home in 1833—

stepped in. He bought a rocky, malodorous piece of land at an extortionary price and constructed the first wet dock on the western coast of India. 'It was a stupendous work,' wrote Cecil Roth in *The Sassoon Dynasty*. 'It took three years to complete, from 1872 to 1875, and it covered an area of little less than 200,000 square feet.'

Later, the Bombay Port Trust bought Sassoon Dock and used it as a 'trooping dock'. Which is how it came about that Winston Churchill had the famous accident that changed the course of his life—and possibly that of world history. Churchill was a junior officer when he was shipped to Bombay in 1896. 'We came alongside of a great stone wall with dripping steps and iron rings for hand-holds,' Churchill wrote later about his misadventure at Sassoon Dock. 'The boat rose and fell four or five feet with the surges. I put out my hand and grasped at a ring; but before I could get my feet on the steps the boat swung away, giving my right shoulder a sharp and peculiar wrench.' Churchill had torn the capsular attachments of his shoulder joint. The injury ensured that he used a pistol instead of a sword in the unexpectedly deadly Battle of Omdurman in Sudan. That saved his life, which in turn almost certainly had an impact on the outcome of World War II, as well.

This little port with a big history is now the city's seafood market. During the day it is thick with fishy smells and fishier drips. But, one day, venture into the dock in the quiet hours of the evening, when the sun is setting and the fishing boats are gliding homewards over unruffled, topaz waters and it's possible to catch a glimpse of the island that once was. Before ships and docks and blocky buildings made it their home.

Saurab Rao

Present-day Sassoon Dock.

Even while Sassoon Dock was being built, most of the action was taking place on the other side of the sprawling Cotton Green. In 1865, an elegant neo-classical fountain was erected to greet the visitors who spilled out of ships and steamers at the Apollo Bunder. The fountain was named after the Duke of Wellington—the English general who eventually defeated Napoleon in the Battle of Waterloo. The Duke of Wellington had served in India (and danced with our old acquaintance Mrs Hough), and the fountain was erected on the approximate spot where his tent was pitched during his two visits in 1801 and 1804.

The slender memorial stands in the middle of one of the busiest cross-streets in the city today, which makes it tough to spot the cast iron leaves at the top and the marble statues along the octagonal base. The best views are from the slight elevation of the city's BEST buses, so next time keep your eyes peeled.

The memorial to the Duke of Wellington was the first of many projects in the area. Just beyond the fringes of Colaba, the Europeans-only Watson's Hotel was constructed using a pre-fab cast iron frame that was shipped all the way from England. The hotel was so popular that an annex later came up near the Yacht Club in Colaba. But the death of the owner John Watson, the hotel's illiberal policies and the arrival of the Taj Mahal Hotel lead to its eventual demise

After Watson's Hotel shut down, the cast-iron-framed building was subdivided into tiny cubby holes. These were used by lawyers and small businesses. As a schoolgirl, I was a loyal patron of 'Smart and Hollywood', the 'costumiers and outfitters' that occupied a room on the ground floor. Two masterjis, head tailors, manned the front desk. Behind them sat about eight tailors, cutting and sewing away. And behind the tailors were two changing rooms from which emerged an unpredictable procession of glitter-gowned

Miss Indias, gauzy butterflies, pastel pixies and gloved and hatted memsahibs.

As much as the masterjis were keepers of fashion, they were keepers of morals and propriety—as I found out to my great exasperation. I once asked 'Smart and Hollywood' to make me a mini skirt for a college social. In the fifteen minutes that it took me to get home, the masterji had already phoned my mother and completed a high-level pow wow. It came as no surprise then that I was stuck with the longest mini skirt in the history of St Xavier's College socials.

Years later, as a journalist I ventured deeper into the crumbling, twilit hotel to meet lawyers in the bowels of the second floor. This involved walking on rotting wooden staircases past dark rooms from which rustles, thumps and syringes routinely emerged. (Today the building is shrouded in nets and scaffolding, and even the most desperate squatters have left. The masterjis who outfitted fairies and fashionistas since 1942 have found a temporary home in Colaba.)

Watson's Hotel was still in its heydays when Mark Twain visited Bombay in 1895. It was on one of the cast iron balconies that the American writer became acquainted with the cheerful Bombay crow—'the product of immemorial ages, and of deep calculation; one can't make a bird like that in a day'.

Watson's Hotel in the 19th century.
Source: Wikimedia Commons.

Twain described his encounter in *Following the Equator*:

If I sat on one end of the balcony, the crows would gather on the railings at the other end and talk about me; and edge closer, little by little, till I could almost reach them; and they would sit there, in the most unabashed way, and talk about my clothes, and my hair and my complexion and probable character and vocation and politics, and how I came to be in India, and what I was doing, and how many days I had got for it, and how I had happened to go unhanged so long, and when would it probably come off, and might there be more of my sort where I came from, and when would they would be hanged—and so on and

> so on, until I could no longer endure the embarrassment of it; then I would shoo them away, and they would circle around in the air a little while, laughing and deriding and mocking, and presently settle on the rail and do it all over again.

(I know, I know. I'm cheating. By my own rules, Watson's Hotel does not belong in Colaba. But the crows that visited Mark Twain a century ago behave uncannily like the crows outside my window. They could well have been Colaba crows…that's my first excuse. My second is that the Watson's Hotel Annexe was in Colaba. It stood where Dhanraj Mahal stands now. So it is a Colabawala of sorts.)

Other than the cacophonic chorus of crows, the guests at the swish hotel must have had to put up with a great deal of banging and hammering. All over Colaba, projects were being executed, turrets and domes erected, and dreams realized. The BB and CI Magazine talks about the 'towering structures caged in scaffolding that had already cut off the view of the old Fort and the clamour of labourers and the "click, click, click" of the stonedresser's chisel'.

I picture the Colaba of those years as a time-lapse video, with familiar structures popping up one by one, filling the empty spaces and creating a familiar streetscape:

1865—The Wellington Fountain
1872—Colaba Station
1874—The stables and offices of the Bombay Tramway Company

1876—The Royal Alfred Sailor's Home
1881—The Yacht Club
1897—The Yacht Club Annexe
1902—The Taj Mahal Palace
1905—The Wodehouse Church
1909—Majestic Hotel
1914—The Museum
1924—The Gateway of India
1934—Regal Cinema

Even in 1876, passengers, after disembarking at Apollo Bunder and picking their way through bundles of opium and cotton, confronted open land under an unfettered sky. Which was why the construction of the chunky, stone structure, the Royal Alfred Sailor's Home, was such an event in the city. Meant as a moderately priced hostel for seamen, it was designed by F.W. Stevens, the genius behind Victoria Terminus station, now known as Chhatrapati Shivaji Maharaj Terminus. 'He cast his design for this Sailor's Home in the Gothic, and to give the building appropriate expression; to give it a fitting nautical touch, he adorned the pediment with a sculpted figure of Neptune,' the BB and CI Magazine exclaims. 'All Bombay gazed at the work, and as it fronted the open space that extended all the way to Back Bay, it must have been viewed with much curiosity by travelers arriving from the north by the trains of the newly-opened BB and CI Railways.'

It would have contributed greatly to the enjoyment of the gawkers and to the nightmares of the resident sailors to know that this structure stood on notorious ground. For it was built over the graves of Mendham's Point—that insatiable cemetery that had swallowed innumerable British lives before it was razed in 1762.

An archival image of The Sailor's Home.
Source: British Library.

The Sailor's Home opened in 1876 and housed sailors for half a century. Its most noteworthy guest was Joseph Conrad, the Polish sailor-novelist, whose *Heart of Darkness* remains one of the most disturbing, ambiguous books ever written. Conrad found himself ashore and unemployed in Madras after he had a spat with his ship's captain. He made his way to Bombay and, while he was looking for a job, stayed at the Sailor's Home.

One day, while sitting on the veranda, he saw a graceful ship slide into the harbour. This was the *Narcissus*. A few days later, Conrad had become her second mate and the six months he spent on the ship are the foundation for his book, *The Nigger of the Narcissus*.

Colaba Station was built in 1872. Just down the road, the Bombay Tramway Company started running horse-drawn trams in the city in 1874. The first route connected Colaba with Crawford Market and Pydhonie. And approximately where Electric House stands today, the company maintained a stable with hundreds of horses.

These stables became a bone of contention in 1900, when the city's Catholics felt that their chapel in Medows Street was inadequate. Archbishop Dalhoff decided that it was time to build a big, new church, away from the crowds and commotion of Fort. He approached the Bombay Improvement Trust for 'two plots of ground between the Wodehouse Road and the Elphinstone College Students' Boarding House' to build a church, a priests' residence and a school.

At first the Trust offered the Archbishop a plot behind the Tramway Station. (Somewhere, I imagine, across from turreted Buckley Court.) The Archbishop protested that the new site was mingy and that the proximity of the stables would be 'obnoxious'. He also stated that the racket of the trams would distract worshippers—and, in general, indicated that the site was unworthy of the high purpose for which it was meant.

After much backing and forthing, the Catholic church

acquired Plots 8, 9 and 10 on Wodehouse Road. My school, Fort Convent, was the first of the buildings to be completed in 1904—setting the stage for generations of maidens in ungainly beige sacks; for innumerable perusals of the fat, daunting grammar book called *Wren and Martin*; and for countless renditions of our virtuous school song that urged us 'on paths of duty / lifting us beyond the skies / where God dwells and ever loves us…'

Then on 15 January 1905, the Church of the Holy Name Cathedral was opened and blessed. And for the first time its four bells pealed alongside bells of the Bhid Bhanjan Mahadev Mandir in Colaba. The *Examiner* describes the ringing of the bells as 'not altogether with that perfect manipulation which can only be acquired by practice, but sufficiently well to show their musical power'.

Over a 100 years later, of course, practice has made perfect. The bells are part of the Colaba soundscape, and the Cathedral of the Holy Name is part of every self-respecting clue-hunt in town. After all, where else in Mumbai would you find a fierce dragon? Or a charming widow brandishing the decapitated head of her enemy? Or, for that matter, a bell named Paulina?

Spend some time here and you will find a sense of serenity, as well as an array of eye-popping stories. Some of these unfold on the ruby-and-sapphire-hued stained-glass windows. Others on the golden, vaulted ceilings. While still others are hidden amid the memorial slabs and tombs that dot this lovely church. There is Saint George who rescued a princess from a plague-bearing, children-devouring dragon, and Judith who chopped off the head of an Assyrian general to save her people.

And, of course, the long-forgotten Bombayites: Dona Rufina Angelice, Relict of the late comendador Jose Correa Aguiarde Aguiar of Oporto; Millicent Eileen Helen, the beloved daughter of Mr and Mrs J.R. Goodser who died when she was just thirteen.

Designed by W.A. Chambers, the foundation stone of this neo-gothic church was laid in 1902 to sonorous Gregorian chants and general satisfaction. Statues of the saints were acquired in Munich and elaborate windows were made of Munich glass. Incredibly, the glowing frescoes that cover the ceiling with Biblical scenes were all executed by a single Italian priest, Brother Moscheni of Bergamo, in just a year. St George and St Theodore bagged pride of place in the church, as they were patron saints of the first two archbishops of Bombay, George Porter and Theodore Dalhoff.

While the Bombay Improvement Trust—which had been set up in 1898, in the wake of the plague epidemic—was parcelling out land along Wodehouse Road, there was much activity on the other side of Colaba Causeway where reclamation had yielded 43 acres. Substantial buildings with wide windows and lofty ceilings appeared along Mandlik Road and Henry Road, Garden Road and Ormiston Road.

With Sargent House and Sunny House and Candy House came middle-class families.

And, ironically, a club house from which they would remain barred all the way till 1947.

Today the Yacht Club is an idiosyncratic remnant of the Raj. But at its peak it was the 'rendezvous of all rank and fashion in Bombay'. Housed in a low, pretty structure built along the sea front, it was where military wives went for high tea and a bracing diatribe against the 'natives'. Where the stuffy, discriminatory hierarchies of the Raj held sway and little romances were enacted amidst the evening shadows on the lawn. (The ships in the harbour had been instructed not to shine their searchlights on the Yacht Club lawn after dark, for fear that they would reveal too many secrets.)

'Here, in the cool of the evening, the people gather to take tea at the little tables set along the sea wall, for the Yacht Club lawn juts out into the waters of the harbor,' wrote Margaret Peterson in *Just Because*. 'In one corner of the lawn the bands of the regiment take it in turn to play day and day about; businessmen look in late of an evening for bridge or scandal; harassed civilians call to collect their wives after office; the young men drop in after polo or some such strenuous game to shed the light of their presence on the expectant and welcoming fair sex. And outside the club precincts, gathered together on the Apollo Bunder, are the carriages of the humbler folk, the non-members of the club, the Parsee and Eurasian community. Outside the pale they can still enjoy the music and amuse themselves by watching society disport itself on the lawns.'

Peterson's fictional account is infuriating, but it mirrors an even more appalling reality. 'Like other clubs and hotels at that time, the membership was restricted exclusively to Europeans,' write Sharda Dwivedi and Rahul Mehrotra in *Fort Walks*. 'According to one tale, although a wealthy Parsi magnate with an English wife donated an expensive billiard table to the Club, he was never permitted to enter.'

Saurab Rao

The Yacht Club Annexe concealed many naughty stories and secret liaisons.

The low, sea-fronting structure that was once the Yacht Club—the setting for dances and discrimination—is now used for the offices of the Department of Atomic Energy and the club functions out of what was once its own residential annex. It still makes delicious Christmas ham and pudding and serves a stuffed suckling pig for its Christmas buffet. Even today it exudes a wistfulness for times past—and actually flew the British flag on its ramparts till the mid-1990s.

The purported story of the Taj Mahal Hotel is a welcome antidote to that of the Yacht Club. It's believed that Jamsetji Tata decided to build a splendid hotel after he was refused admission to a 'Europeans Only' hostelry in the city. Whether this satisfying tit-for-tat tale is true or not, Jamsetji tackled his new project with unmatched zeal. 'Unlike his other enterprises, Jamsetji did not calculate what it would cost. He bought reclaimed land at Apollo Bunder and started building,' wrote R.M. Lala in *The Creation of Wealth*. 'The Gateway was yet to be built. There, facing the mouth of the harbor, the Taj rose in its solitary grandeur.'

That the hotel turned its back to the sea surprised many of its European guests and threw up yet another legend. This one claimed that a British architect had designed the Taj to face the sea. When he returned to Bombay after a long absence, he was stricken to find that it had been built the wrong way and proceeded to fling himself from the top floor in a fitting finale.

Although this tale is as delectable as the cold coffee ice cream at the Sea Lounge, it's not true. Khanderao Sitaram and D.N. Mirza were the original architects of the Taj—and they deliberately oriented the hotel so that its rooms could benefit from the westerly breezes.

Jamsetji Tata was involved in the tiniest details. He bought elaborate equipment, including a soda and ice-making machine from the US, chandeliers from Berlin and pillars of spun iron from Paris to hold up the ballroom. He warned his son to 'avoid the abominable yellows and reds' in the décor. He even bought two small islands near Uran called Panjoo and Dongri so that his guests could picnic there.

The hotel cost a whopping Rs 25 lakh, and Jamsetji's contemporaries sneeringly referred to it as 'Tata's White Elephant'. Even his doting family was skeptical. R.M. Lala recounted that when Jamsetji told them about his new venture, his sister remonstrated, 'What? You want to build a science institute in Bangalore, a great iron and steel factory, a hydro-electric plant and now a Battarkhana (eating place)?'

What few people realized was that the Taj was fated to become a Battarkhana like no other. Over the years it has hosted celebrities ranging from actor Gregory Peck to romance writer Barbara Cartland; playwright George Bernard Shaw to author Somerset Maugham. There was the time when John Lennon and Yoko Ono locked themselves in the Rajput Suite for five days and asked not to be disturbed; and the time when Duke Ellington jammed in the Grand Ballroom. Not to forget the numerous occasions when Ruttie Jinnah stormed into the Taj after flaming rows with her husband, Mohammed Ali Jinnah.

Even so, the early years were wobbly. The hotel announced itself with a quiet newspaper advertisement: 'Taj Mahal Palace Hotel, Bombay. Open 1st December, 1903. All Latest Comforts. Moderate Charges. From Rs. 6 upwards.' Only seventeen guests availed of the offer and business remained slow. The Bombay of those days was a troubled city, grappling with the plague and land-reclamation schemes gone bust. European visitors were wary of the Moorish vibe and mixed company. Then Indian princes, always happy to party and guzzle beer in merry Bombay, began sauntering in with their bejewelled entourages and pet tigers. They kept the hotel afloat.

Louis Bromfield provides a vivid description of those wild, early days in his novel, set in the 1920s, *Night in Bombay*:

> In those days the Taj Mahal Hotel had the air of a vast and dreary country jail. Built around two or three great wells which ran the full height of the building, the stairs were of stone and the railings of iron, and around the great wells ran galleries, likewise with stone floors and iron railings. Off these the rooms opened, each one more like a cell than a hotel room, each specifically furnished with an iron bed, covered with netting and with a single hard mattress, a washstand and a couple of stiff, uncomfortable chairs.
>
> Overhead there was a large, old-fashioned electric punkah, and outside on the cool slate floors slept the bearers. They slept there not only at night but all through

the hot days, when they were not gossiping with other bearers. The jail-like corridors were as much an exchange place of gossip as any market place. The bearers from one end to the other of the vast hotel knew everything about every guest in the hotel, his vices, his peculiarities, his meanesses or generosities. It was as if each room were walled with glass for all the world to look inside.

And downstairs on the ground floor there was a vast hall and a huge stairway which lead up and up into the heights of the great hotel. Through the hall and the bazaar that occupied half its area came and went a procession of Arab horse dealers, British Governors and civil servants, Russian and German trollops, Indian princes, jewel merchants, Parsi millionaires, comic middle aged tourists, gamblers, oil-prospectors. The procession went on day and night, for in the heat of the city and with the fantastic character of many of the guests, the place was as alive at four in the morning as at midday.

In the 1970s, the modern, new wing of the Taj came up, where once had stood Green's Hotel, another colourful Colaba institution. 'Green's Restaurant fifty years ago was the place where you could enjoy P & O cold store haddocks and kippers, a great treat then,' wrote H. Hobbs in *John Barleycorn Bahadur*, a book on the taverns of India. 'Many would willingly have paid a couple of rupees for that tasty breakfast dish so there was a great crowd in Green's when the mail steamer was in.'

In the Roaring '20s and Swinging '30s, however, the crowd that frequented Green's was unlikely to surface in time for breakfast. The big draws by this point were the amateur music nights and Saturday dances. 'The swing bands had a lot to do with creating Green's raffish appeal,' wrote Naresh Fernandes in *Taj Mahal Foxtrot*. 'By 1924, the dances at Green's were always packed, as were similar events across the city.'

When the sun dipped beneath the horizon and all you could see were the lights of approaching boats, alluring women shimmied into the restaurant, smiled upon unattached males and put up tantalizing shows with names like 'Dance of the Seven Veils'. Bromfield described the moonlit terrace and the 'hard girls on the verge of middle age from Hove and Cardiff and Liverpool and London whom some strange fate had dumped into Bombay as sleazy tap dancers and members of a ladies' orchestra. And here and there a stray Russian tart or and "advanced" Parsi or Khoja woman, dining alone with a man'.

It's strange to imagine my grandmother, living 50 metres away, staring at the same fat, rich moon and listening to the same tram clatter by. It seems almost impossible to reconcile her world with this world of swing bands and cabarets. But then, more and more, I'm realizing that the Colaba of the early 1900s had more layers than even the Dance of the Seven Veils.

There was the strict, middle-class realm within which

my grandparents functioned; the ancient Koli villages that dotted the coast; the clamorous bazaars with their golden fruits, silver shops and rumours; the Cotton Green where millionaires plotted their rise; the 'chhota peg and burra sahib' world of the Yacht Club and Watson's Hotel; the insouciant bubble of floaters, dancers and gamblers who drifted through the city in beaded dresses, bobbed hair and Clark Gable moustaches. And, of course, the cantonment that was a constant reminder of the might of the Empire.

As was the city's most recognizable symbol of colonialism: the Gateway of India, built to commemorate the visit of King George V in 1911. George Wittet, the architect who undertook ninety-five major projects for the city and who now lies in an overgrown corner of the Sewri cemetery, drew up an elaborate plan. This began with the reclamation of a chunk of land, the construction of a sea wall and the building of the yellow basalt Gateway itself.

Inscription on the gateway reading: 'Erected to commemorate the landing in India of their Imperial Majesties King George V and Queen Mary on the Second of December MCMXI'. *Source: Wikimedia Commons.*

Once this was completed, Wittet had planned a grand avenue that extended all the way from the Gateway to the Wellington Fountain. As this would have meant demolishing roads and buildings—including the Yacht Club annexe—it's understandable that the project was aborted after the Gateway was completed in 1924. Still, the original plans allow us to imagine an alternate Mumbai—and explain why the Gateway stands at an odd angle, always seeming a tad lost and confused, like a tourist who has strayed away from his guide.

It's a rare visitor—either very evolved or very lazy—who will leave the city without a photograph at the Gateway of India. I'm not a tourist in Colaba, which is why I don't have a single picture. What I do have, however, are memories of the salty-sweaty evenings of toddlerhood spent under those exquisitely carved arches, eating chana, chasing pigeons, watching the 'time-pass' vendors and the boats rocking on blue-grey waters.

On other evenings I was dispatched to the crescent-shaped lawns of the city's museum, where I became great friends with the ancient stone Buddhas that dot the garden. It was much later that I realized that the Gateway and Museum were siblings. That both were designed by Wittet in a daring fusion of Indian and Western styles.

These two structures were considered his masterpieces, which is ironic given that Wittet was a purist. The consulting architect to the government of Bombay didn't approve of the Indo-Saracenic fashion that had seized the city and he proposed a classical design for the city's new museum. Eventually, he had to succumb to the wishes of the museum committee, which held the purse-strings. Wittet's design—with its pearly dome, Rajasthani jharokas, Islamic arches and wooden pavilion from a wada in Nasik—is breathtakingly audacious. 'The real reason why it is so, is because it was instructed that the design should be Indian in character,' Wittet later remarked a trifle sourly. Wittet needn't have been grumpy. I'm all for artistic integrity, but I have to admit that this time the Mr Moneybags were right.

Not all those who attempted Indo-Gothic edifices in Colaba were equally successsful, however. The Majestic Hotel—which opened in 1909 with ninety-six bedrooms, two lifts, Italian management and a popular dance band—could well have auditioned for the part of Bluebeard's castle. And somehow its 'enter at your own risk' demeanour was enhanced by the addition of frivolous turrets and crenellations.

'The architecture of the Majestic and the Taj Mahal Hotel is not described in the guidebook,' that most acerbic of writers, Aldous Huxley, remarked in 1926. 'It is a remissness; they deserve description. The Majestic is more wildly Mahommedan than the most orthodox of Great Mughals ever dreamed of, and the gigantic Taj combines the style of the South Kensington Museum with that of an Indian Pavilion at an International Exhibition.'

The Majestic remains a brooding presence along Colaba Causeway, but has mutated into a hostel for MLAs. The

An old postcard featuring Majestic Hotel and the Waterloo Mansion. *Source: oldphotosbombay.blogspot.com.*

large foyer that once featured potted palms, deep armchairs and reading lamps under which Englishmen perused *The Times of India*, is now a vast department store. And the ghouls that most certainly inhabit this gloomy edifice have probably been defanged and declawed by the much scarier MLAs who lurk the higher floors; and by the whiffs of bleach and overripe papayas from the Sahakari Bhandar downstairs. (As someone who spent a substantial chunk of her childhood in those grey, whiffy aisles, I can only sympathize.)

By 1914, the ring of buildings around Wellington Fountain was almost complete. There was the Sir Cowasji Jehangir Hall that is now the National Gallery of Modern Art. The pearly domed museum. The Royal Alfred Sailor's Home. The Majestic Hotel. And, finally, Waterloo Mansion.

Waterloo Mansion was the only residential building in this exclusive club. It was built by the Maharajah of Morvi and, for a brief spell, was home to one of the most fascinating characters from the age of intrigue and espionage—the mysterious Alexander Malcolm Jacob, businessman, swindler, spy and magician.

Through the 1880s, Mr Jacob ran an old curiosity shop located on Shimla's famous Mall. Nobody quite knew whether he was an Armenian, a Pole, a Turk, a Greek or a gypsy. Nobody knew if he truly possessed occult powers and could actually walk on water. Or whether he really controlled a network of spies that extended all the way to the Hindu Kush. Still, the incredible Mr Jacob was so compelling that Rudyard Kipling used him and his shop as the inspiration for Lugan Sahib's School for Spies in his Great Game novel, *Kim*.

When this 'intelligent, indefatigable bric-a-brac hunter' heard about the discovery of a magnificent diamond called the Imperial in the mines of South Africa, he cobbled together a daring plan. He decided that he would buy the gem for Rs 21 lakh and sell it for Rs 50 lakh. 'The customer that Jacob would groom to buy the stone was Mahboob Ali Khan, the opium-addicted, incredibly wealthy sixth Nizam,' wrote John Zubrzycki in *The Mysterious Mr Jacob: Diamond Merchant, Magician and Spy*. 'The transaction set an unbroken record for the highest price ever paid for a single gem and triggered the most sensational case to come before the Calcutta High Court in decades.'

Mr Jacob started by whetting the appetite of the Nizam of Hyderabad for this magnificent diamond and convinced him to transfer Rs 23 lakh so that the diamond could be transported to India. The diamond arrived and was presented to Mahboob Ali Khan on a silver tray covered with red velvet. Then, just when everything was going swimmingly, the capricious Nizam veered from the script. He picked up the flashing gem and announced, 'Na pasand.' In that single moment, the deal collapsed. The outcome was a messy court case that destroyed the antique dealer. The diamond finally went to the Nizam who, convinced that it was unlucky, stowed it away in an old shoe for his son to find years later.

In 1903, Mr Jacob moved to No. 9 Waterloo Mansion where he lived in a flat overlooking the Wellington Fountain and continued to sell curios to tourists. His flat was right above the shop that is today occupied by the famous Philips Antiques—another wonderful Colaba coincidence.

There was one last plot that overlooked Wellington Fountain. It was occupied by an old saluting battery, used occasionally to greet visiting dignitaries. In 1920, this was removed and the land was leased to two Parsi businessmen. They, in turn, commissioned Charles Stevens—the son of the legendary F.W. Stevens—to design a cinema hall.

Incredibly, Regal Cinema did not succumb to peer pressure. Although it stands alongside so many Bombay Gothic worthies, it does not possess a single cupola or cornice. Stevens adopted an uncompromising Art Deco style that captured the derring-do of the city's first air-conditioned theatre, with its underground parking lot and snazzy soda fountain.

Regal started its celluloid career with a Laurel and Hardy comedy in 1933. The early patrons were delighted, not just by the antics of the daffy duo, but with the various elegancies and novelties—ice cream served in wine glasses, an elevator that whooshed up from the underground parking lot. As were future generations of Colabaites who snuck into Regal on blazing afternoons, bought a packet of plump samosas and journeyed to the Red Sea in Biblical times, or to a village in Haryana, or to a galaxy far, far away.

That the theatre is struggling and may close down is a heartbreaking thought. For, as any Colabaite will vouch, the magic of this corner of Mumbai is about much more than cement and stone. It is about the time that Gregory Peck popped into Regal to see how his film *Twelve O'Clock High* was doing. And about Rabindranath Tagore reciting his poetry and Yehudi Menuhin playing his violin on its stage.

It is about Café Mondegar—Mondy's to supercilious regulars—which started life as a basic Irani restaurant but has repackaged itself as a happening bar and eatery that features murals by Mario Miranda, Colaba's most famous cartoonist.

It is about Café Leopold, which opened for business in 1871, and changed with the times from warehouse to general store to an eatery so seedy that my grandmother forbade me to ever walk past it. To finally a multi-cuisine tourist magnet that—after the terrorist attacks of 26/11 that left five customers and two waiters dead—has become an unexpected symbol of the city's resilience.

It is about Olympia Coffee House and Stores, which has remained faithful to the 100-year-old recipes of its original Iranian owners, and still serves up the most flavourful biryani, bheja fry, paya and kheema-pav.

It is about Rajsi Bros, Grand Bazaar and Khubsons that filled their windows with plaster mannequins, furry blankets and floral cotton textiles. And Farm Products, the city's oldest cold storage that has been run by the Rochas since 1890, and continues to supply Colaba with sausages and chops. Not to forget turkey stuffed with pork mince, cranberries and green apples at Christmas.

It is about the first radio broadcast in India that was made in 1923 by the Radio Club of Bombay. And about the spirited card parties that 90-year-old Kamla Lalwani recalls playing in the club. And about the fishermen's wharf that the club replaced. (All that remains of that wharf is, apparently, the original gate, which has now been incorporated into the nearby temple. Must try and find it.)

It is about Nanking and Fredriks, that brought honey-glazed pork spareribs, Singapore crabs and chopsticks to Colaba. And about Bhang's and Florence and Blue Heaven Beauty Parlour, that ushered in the era of manicures and sleek haircuts.

It's about mysterious dealers in antiques, who may or may not have commanded supernatural forces and a network of spies. About the Koli fishermen who still venture into the plastic-filled seas, and about women from faraway villages who sweep and iron and stir and make sure that this city wakes up and eats and wears clean clothes.

It is about early experiments with theatre in Colaba buildings. And Goan musicians who flocked to the city to play in swing bands. Malcolm Raymond, the jazz pianist at Ali Baba. Frank Fernand, the trumpeter who performed with a multinational band at the Majestic. Chic Chocolate, the trumpeter and bandleader, who managed to squeeze two pianos and one family into his single-bedroom apartment in Colaba.

The aroma of biryani, the toot of the trumpets, the clamour of many tongues were the backdrop against which larger events unfolded. The birth of the Indian National Congress. The inexplicable epidemic of plague that devastated the city. The deadly arrival of the Spanish Flu. Crime. War.

As Bombay changed, so did Colaba. First the docks moved away. Then the Cotton Green. And, finally, Colaba Station.

By 1920, it seemed pointless to lug mountains of cotton all the way to the southern tip of Bombay just to carry the same mountains away to the new docks and the new cotton mills of Parel and Dadar. In 1923, the Cotton Green moved to Sewri.

After which Colaba Station seemed redundant, even inconvenient. 'The Backbay project was pursued wholeheartedly and the railways were asked to close their line between Churchgate and Colaba. On the New Year's morning of 1931, the BB and CI track finally terminated at Churchgate as the previous night on Dec 31, 1930, Colaba was closed down,' wrote Mr Aklekar in *Halt Station India*. But does anything remain of that station with the arches, rose windows and sloping roof? 'If you go to Badhwar Park,' Mr Aklekar promises, 'you will find some original railings and a tree from the old station.'

Paltry though these relics seem, I am determined to find them. But it does seem that the BB and CI magazine was right when it stated that 'the man who rang the bell for the last departure rang a great change of sixty years for Colaba...'

(Colaba lesson for life—Don't pin all your hopes on one diamond.)

8. The Birth of a Neighbourhood

'At one point of time, we believed that the people who lived in Colaba were more cultured and refined. Though I wouldn't say that that is valid today.

'The Colaba of our days was a very different, quiet place. When I was six or seven years old, my ayah used to take me to the promenade for a morning walk. I remember telling my mother with amazement, "Today eighteen cars passed me!"'

—Jimmy Baria has spent eighty years in Jony Castle, which was originally built as a maternity home in the old Cuffe Parade area.

THE COLABA OF THE 1930S WAS A WORK IN PROGRESS—AN embryonic neighbourhood that, over the next couple of decades, gradually rose out of the old Cotton Green, the dismantled railway station and, of course, the sea.

The Times of India directory indicates that even in 1932, the southern stretch of Colaba Causeway was a mix of vacant plots, railway offices and godowns. While the more happening northern stretch featured dressmakers, milliners, florists and restaurants that reeked of 'back home' nostalgia: Union Jack Restaurant, Piccadilly Restaurant, Ladies' Shorthand Typewriting Institute, Misses Miranda Milliners and Dressmakers, New English Dairy, Yvonne Dressmaker.

Change, however, was in the air. Buildings like Kulsum Terrace and Glamour sprang up where once were cotton bales, warehouses and open maidans.

Edifices, some Art Deco, other basic buildings-in-a-hurry, rose along the four Pasta Lanes near the bazaar. Before you start imagining a culinary back story, the Pasta Lanes were not named after penne and fusilli. They were named after a cotton merchant named Sheth Mohanjee who was granted the title of Pasta or Prince because of his generosity.

The serene, butter-cream Parsi colony of Cusrow Baug replaced the railway yard. It was built by the Wadias, the prominent ship-building family that constructed 355 vessels over 160 years, and today runs Bombay Dyeing and GoAir.

Cusrow Baug brought patra ni machhi, dhansaak and nankhatai bands (the small brass bands that regaled the Parsi community) to Colaba. It brought fierce old women who lay in wait for wall-climbing, shortcut-taking children. And

Swabal stores with its sugarcane vinegars, prawn patias and terrifyingly grouchy cashier, who sat on a raised platform and reigned over his domain. ('Do I look like I want your money?' he once roared at me when I had the temerity to hand him a twenty-rupee note instead of Rs 19.95. I had to return ten minutes later with a plastic bag full of 5 and 10 paisa coins and a pounding, twelve-year-old heart.)

The Colaba Parsis were—at least according to the city's most beloved columnist, Busybee—a distinct species. 'There are Colaba Parsis, Tardeo Parsis and Dadar Parsi Colony Parsis,' he wrote. 'The Colaba Parsis work in advertising agencies, act in Hosi Vasunia's plays and have relations in Toronto. The Tardeo Parsis would like to be Colaba Parsis. The Dadar Parsi Colony Parsis are Dadar Parsi Colony Parsis.'

While the Colaba Parsis were becoming Colaba Parsis, builders and house-hunters were venturing further south towards Sassoon Dock and beyond. To that skinny strip of land that was once just wilderness and two whitewashed tombs. Road by road, building by building, big city aspirations swallowed the past.

It was only in the military area that the Colaba of history books and travellers' accounts could be glimpsed. Even today, few people have reason to venture into that remote corner of the city. Perhaps an invitation for a wedding at the Colaba Agiary. A desire to drop in at one of the flower-bedecked dargahs of Sufi saints who supposedly came to isolated Colaba from Baghdad many centuries ago. A school trip to the overgrown compound that houses the Met office. Or a lecture at the Tata Institute of Fundamental Research (TIFR).

TIFR, the country's most important hub of scientific research, was founded by physicist Homi Bhabha in his childhood home on Peddar Road in 1945. It moved to the old Yacht Club near Apollo Bunder a few years later. And then to the foamy rim of Colaba—a windswept plot that Prime Minister Jawaharlal Nehru helped prise from the reluctant Ministry of Defence. In 1962, a spanking new institute filled with Bhabha's art collection and enthusiasm took its place in the world of science.

Despite the occasional intrusions, however, Upper Colaba remained a place of majestic trees, quiet bungalows and high security—quite unlike the rest of Bombay that was hurrying towards its future.

In the 1930s, buildings were being built, businesses were being established and parties being held. The terraces, streets and bars of Colaba were at the heart of the action—and witnessed a parade of adventurers, chancers, cabaret dancers and musicians. In *Trumpet Story*, Bill Coleman recalled his six-month-long sojourn on Garden Road. Coleman was invited, along with a group of musicians, to perform at the Taj. This included the pianist, Charles 'Dizzy' Lewis, who overdid the booze one afternoon and then wandered onto the street where he befriended a snake-charmer:

> Dizzy bought a python and took it home. No one was there when Dizzy arrived and the juice started getting Dizzy down, so he got on a bed with the python and went to sleep. When his girlfriend Ivy came home, the sight that she saw sent her out of the house screaming like mad. Dizzy was lying on his back with his mouth wide open. The python was coiled around his body and its head was five inches from his mouth. The alcohol from his breath must have paralyzed the python to the point where it could not squeeze the life out of him. Ivy went to get her brother and, with the help of some friends they got the python into a cloth bag and gave it to the zoo.

The mad, merry times continued into World War II. Bombay was an ideal stopover for Allied soldiers heading to the East. It was also considered the perfect spot for rest and recuperation. 'In 1942, Japan joined the war,' recalled activist B.C. Dutt in a piece written for a marvellous booklet on Colaba, brought out by the India Heritage Society. 'Colaba, having the barracks there, the Causeway was full of uniforms. The British, Australians, Canadians with a sprinkling of Americans, one didn't spot too many Indians.'

The bars of Colaba had never been livelier. There was open-air dancing on the Causeway. Restaurants like Olympia and Leopold offered an 'Army Dish' or a 'Navy Dish' on the menu. Raunchy cabarets and pavement pornography were in great demand. This enraged the authorities of the church, who ranted against 'booksellers who exploit the moral vulnerability of men just come ashore, desperately tired, suffering from high nervous tensions, seeking relief from strain of mind and body'.

Naturally, this was also high season for the 'naughty ladies of Colaba'. 'Many of the Shirleys and Yolandas packed off when the British left,' wrote a regretful Minoo Malegam, a self-professed Anglophile in the Indian Heritage Society booklet, 'but even the second-stringers who stayed on made heads turn, especially after sunset.'

Behram Contractor—the journalist behind the Busybee byline—also recalled the time when the bars and eateries of the Causeway were packed with uniforms and displayed V for Victory signs at the entrance. 'I can still identify the whole row of them starting with Swabal Stores, which has survived both time and the onslaught of the post-independence entrepreneurs,' he wrote in the Indian Heritage Society booklet. 'Then moving on to Star Bakery, with its renowned wine biscuits, Ahura Stores, the Italian Faleti's Restaurant, Hygien Hair-dressing Saloon, Dr Daruwalla's dispensary and Kitchenet. Kitchenet was a Goan restaurant, the best there has ever been in Bombay, and the disappearance of which is the only thing I regret. Long after the war was over in the 1960s, it had retained the tin wartime hoardings at its entrance, publicising its catering. A typical hoarding had two British soldiers painted larger than life. They would be talking to each other: "Hey Joe, I'm hungry. Shall we pop into Kitchenet?" "Yes Tom, let us go to Kitchenet and have its mixed grill of sausages, bacon and liver."'

Then the war ended, the soldiers left, and Kitchenet had fewer takers for its mixed grill. Life seemed set to return to its sleepy ways when, quite without warning, the quietest corner of Colaba tossed its historical hand grenade. 'The war ended with a big bang at least in Colaba,' wrote Dutt. 'The Ratings of the Royal Indian Navy mutinied and I was one of them.'

The Naval Uprising of 1946 began with a group of sailors in Colaba protesting against horrible living conditions, bad food and the supercilious attitudes of British officers. In December 1945, the sailors stationed at the Colaba-based *HMIS Talwar* ripped flags and painted slogans like 'Quit India' and 'Kill the British' on their barracks.

Events snowballed and in February 1946, around 20,000 naval personnel went on strike. Then the millworkers and railway workers went on strike in a show of support. The city was in disarray and 300 people died in riots. The Indian sailors seized control of the naval ships in the Bombay harbour and trained the ships' guns on the Yacht Club, the Gateway of India and the Taj.

The Indian National Congress finally persuaded the sailors to discontinue their strike. But the uprising convinced the British that it was time to go home. Our history textbooks tend to overlook this episode, partly because it was an aberration in the otherwise non-violent movement.

Saurab Rao

Monument dedicated to the naval uprising.

But the Naval Uprising Memorial on Wodehouse Road stands testament to the big part that little Colaba played in the freedom struggle. As does an evocative passage in *The Moor's Last Sigh* by Salman Rushdie:

> When Aurora Zogoiby heard that the Naval Strike Committee had been persuaded by the Congress leadership to call off the stoppage, and that it had convoked a meeting of the sailors to order them back to their posts, her disappointment with the world as it was burst its banks. Without thinking, without waiting for her driver Hanuman, she leapt into the curtained Buick and took off for the naval base. By the time she reached the Afghan Church in the Colaba Cantonment, however, the bubble of her invulnerability had burst, and she was beginning to have second thoughts about the wisdom of her journey. The road to the base was thick with defeated sailors,

frustrated young men in clean uniforms and filthy moods, young men swirling listlessly like fallen leaves. Crows jeered in a plane-tree; a sailor picked up a stone and hurled it in the direction of the noise. Black forms fluttered contemptuously, circled, settled down, resumed their taunts. Police officers in short trousers muttered anxiously in small knots, like children afraid of punishment, and even my mother began to see that this was no place for a lady with a sketchbook and folding stool, let alone a gleaming Buick without so much as the protective presence of a chauffeur. It was a hot, humid, ill-tempered afternoon. A child's lilac kite, its string cut in some other lost battle, fell pathetically from the sky.

Aurora did not need to lower her window to ask what was on the sailors' minds, because she was thinking the same things—that the Congress were acting like chamchas, toadies; that even now, when the British were too unsure of the army to send it in against the sailors, they could be sure that Congresswallahs would spare them the trouble of having to do so.

Fittingly enough, it was from Colaba that the British troops finally departed our shores. On 28 February 1948 they slowly marched through the yellow basalt arches of the Gateway of India and left.

Forever.

Departure of the last British troops from the gateway, in 1948.
Source: Wikimedia Commons.

(Colaba Lesson for Life—Snakes are best handled sober.)

9. My Colaba

'In Karachi we had a huge house with fourteen bedrooms, chandeliers, Persian carpets. We had a carriage, we had a yacht. One evening in 1947, I was playing in the park and I saw the body of a man who had been killed. My father felt that this was a sign. We chartered a flight and came to Bombay, because my mother had two sisters here. For about six months we lived with my aunty in Babulnath, but her house had only two bedrooms and had become very crowded. So my father started searching for a flat, and heard about a building coming up in Colaba called Candy Castle.

'The building was being built by Alyque Padamsee's father for himself and his family, but when he realized that so many immigrants were coming into Bombay, he decided to give out the flats. We booked a flat. Word spread and many well-to-do Sindhis began to move in to Candy Castle and another new building called Mohini. G.P. Sippy, R.J. Advani, Ram Jethmalani all started out in this area. G.P. Sippy shared a small

flat in Candy Castle with thirty people. R.J. Advani—who was the first man to introduce the concept of co-operative housing societies and who built buildings across Colaba—ran a small pakoda stall with his wife in those early days.

'When we moved into Candy Castle, we could see all the way to Apollo Bunder and the lighthouse. In front of us there was open ground and then some garages for government vehicles and a few cottages for the managers. Beyond the garage there were barracks used for communication with the ships at sea. And then a postal colony for postmen in the area.

'When the Sindhis who were well-off came, they realized that this was a very elegant place. The Sindhis from Karachi were used to being near the sea and they found Colaba similar to their home. Also, because it had been inhabited by the British, Colaba was spic and span and not congested at all.

'Slowly the garages and barracks melted away. Almost all the buildings in the area were constructed before our eyes. In those early days, Sindhis set up many small stalls selling kulfi and pani puri and Sindhi mutton. They would wait outside Strand Cinema and bang their pots during the movie interval so that people would come out and eat. It was great fun.'

—Chiku Advani, eighty, witnessed the birth of Little Sind and the transformation of the area around Strand Cinema from open maidans to a bustling residential enclave

By the time I arrived on the scene, the British had long been gone from Colaba. Many others had arrived to take their place.

The Sindhis came after Partition, homesick and heartbroken. They soon discovered Colaba, with its vacant plots and welcoming air. Enterprising Sindhi refugees formed groups, pooled their resources and constructed buildings—including Batra House, where I live.

Besides the concept of the Co-operative Housing Society, they brought chaats, kababs and lotus-root pickles. They set up Hiroo Kebabs, Kailash Parbat and Sindhi Provisions Store. Cheerfully, Colaba accommodated the Little Sind that grew around Strand Cinema.

People from everywhere moved into Cuffe Parade, the controversial reclamation scheme of the 1960s that replaced a beloved promenade and mangroves with skyscrapers. The residents included the artist M.F. Husain, the poet Adil Jussawalla, and the columnist Shobhaa Dé.

Years later, Jussawalla wrote, in *Bombay, Meri Jaan: Writings on Mumbai* edited by Jerry Pinto and Naresh Fernandes, about the accusations and envy that came his way after he moved into a Cuffe Parade high-rise:

It's the eighteenth floor blues. This is how they feel, or something like how they feel—

How do you do
Up there
Just as low as you
Down there
As low as a canoe

Up there
Got the 18th floor blues

The lows began with Mulk
Down there
They said I'd blocked his light
Up there
That started off a fight
Somewhere
And my 18th floor blues

Right next door came people from the dry, drought-wracked villages of Maharashtra, Karnataka and Bihar. They came for jobs, and started living in plastic-and-asbestos huts on land reclaimed, inch by inch. Over the decades, the makeshift shelters gave way to bricks; the memory of water to forgetfulness and furious floods.

In recent times, these slums have given refuge to the famous and the infamous. To an Australian bank robber called Gregory David Roberts who escaped from prison and later wrote a bestseller called *Shantaram*. Today you can take a *Shantaram* tour conducted by the residents of Ambedkar Nagar who figured in the book. Or, if you happen to be Madonna, then you can take a tour conducted by Linbaba/Roberts himself.

The bastis of Colaba also provided anonymous accommodation to eight men who came on recce missions to Bombay in 2008. Later, these men returned with their explosives and AK47s and spread devastation through Colaba—in and around the Taj, Leopold and Nariman House.

Smugglers arrived on the high seas with their illegal cargo—gold, chocolates, cheeses, jars of Tang, RDX, other criminals—and were met by obliging fishing boats that brought the contraband to the shores of Colaba.

Makeshift pavement shops sprang up, selling chappals and hankies and raw mango dipped in chilly-salt powder. Today they are the biggest draw of the Causeway and feature in guidebooks and blogs. Siraj from Jharkhand, Ravinder from Gorakhpur—they keep the city supplied with Minion nighties and unicorn pyjamas; summer dresses and striped palazzos; orange beaded slippers and purple feather earrings.

The hippies wandered into Colaba and hung around near the Salvation Army, Leopold Café and Dipti Drink House in their tattoos, tattered kurtas, matted beards and clouds of marijuana. Whether they found love and happiness on the pavements of Merewether Road and Ormiston Road is not known, but they certainly found hash, harem pants and hair lice.

Members of Mumbai's gay community headed to Gokul and Voodoo, where it was possible to enjoy a drink, dance to loud music and initiate discussions that eventually lead to the magazine *Bombay Dost* and the Humsafar Trust. 'After spending time at Gokul and then at The Walls (a popular cruising area along the Gateway of India promenade) most of us had to get back to the suburbs,' recalled film-maker Sridhar Rangayan in an interview with *Verve*. 'We would take the last train (nicknamed The Maharani Express by the community) from Churchgate to Borivali. Our revelry—singing, dancing, gossiping and laughing—would continue on the train.'

Arab visitors flocked to the city in the monsoons, filling the hotels of Colaba, riding horse-drawn victorias in the pelting rain, shopping for frilly dresses at Olgas and attars at the cut-glass-and-mirror-lined perfume shops. Once again, Colaba was happy to accommodate. Street vendors began stocking labneh alongside Wrigley chewing gum. Restaurants put up signs in Arabic. The shops along Arthur Bunder Road began selling dizzying perfumes and tasselled silk robes. They acquired names like Gulf Spices and Ahmed Trading. And Bombay's Little Arabia was born. Buyers from various parts of the world spent months in the three-star hotels of Colaba, sourcing brightly coloured fabrics and mul skirts in the stores that lined the Causeway. South Africans frequented Rosewood, Gypsy Rose and Rose Collections. Shoppers from Senegal, Kenya, Sudan and the Middle East headed to Rajsi Bros and its ilk.

We all know that the Arabs come to Bombay to see the rains. Well this year, at least so far, there had been no rains and all the Arabs were disappointed and their children kept saying this was no holiday and they would like to go somewhere else.

So, this morning, when all the Arabs got up in their hotel rooms at Taj, Oberoi and Diplomat and saw the rains, their joy knew no bounds and some of them felt as they had felt when they had first discovered oil in their backyards at a time when oil prices were high and the world was being made to pay through its noses for its fuel.

And some of the Arabs rang up the managements of their hotels and thanked them for having provided them with rains. And when the bearers came in with tea and breakfast and buttermilk, they gave them thousand-rupee tips and Seiko wristwatches.

And when the Arab children got up, who like children everywhere get up later than their parents, the adult Arabs took them to the windows and pointed to the grey skies and heavy showers and told them: 'Look, look Rafiq, there are the rains. This is what you came all the way from home to see.'

And the children, for once, forgot to play in the lifts of the Taj and instead went out on the Apollo pier and got wet. And old Arabs had tears in their eyes as they watched the rains. 'Allah has given us oil, but not rains,' they said. But they were happy that the rains had come and they had seen them once again, and their children had seen them once again, and their children's children had seen them for the first time.

And, later in the morning, the Arabs were walking up and down Colaba Causeway in the rains, buying up all the umbrellas, which the shop keepers were selling to them at the pre-fall-in-international-oil-price rates.

So even though it is dark and gloomy and depressing and rainy today, if you see an Arab on the road, wish him 'Have a nice day.' Because that is exactly what he is having.

—*Busybee* in his column, 'Round and About',
8 August 2002

Shivaji, the Maratha warrior king, galloped into Colaba too. His bronze statue stands across the Gateway of India. His name has now been tagged to the city museum.

Tourists from the small towns of India arrived by the tour-busloads. They made a beeline for the Gateway of India. And the Shivaji statue. They bought peanuts and postcards on Apollo Bunder and went for half-hour-long boat rides from the jetty. Wealthy Europeans wandered through the Taj, trying on elegant slippers at Joy Shoes, contemplating a diamond bangle at Gazdar, browsing through coffee table books in Nalanda.

These were the people with whom we shared Colaba. Alongside whom we wandered the bazaar, trying on silver belts at Mangal Palace, buying flower-shaped buttons

The iconic Cafe Mondegar, which marks the beginning of the Colaba Causeway. *Source: Wikimedia Commons*

from Pradhan, and beseeching Janata Stores to source our Geography textbooks before the terminal exams. Amidst whom we cycled on summer mornings and bargained on summer afternoons and had Baida Roti at Bade Miyan's as an impromptu dinner treat.

We took it for granted that Colaba was always full of people from elsewhere. That ours was a space marked by Edward the VIII and Piccadilly; Baghdadi and Kailash Parbat; York House and Porbunder Castle. And that each mismatched element contributed to the vivid collage of the neighbourhood. 'Like great rivers elsewhere, the Causeway could take it all: the disappearance of its European residents and restaurants, the coming of rich refugees from Sind with their gaudy sari shops, the march of the hippies and the Arab invasion, the whores who chased them like camp followers,' wrote Firdaus Kanga in *Trying to Grow*. 'With every tributary the Causeway glittered, more cosmopolitan, more gay than any street in India.'

This ability to absorb and accept extended beyond the Causeway and into the by-lanes with their lovely Jaiji Mansions and Broacha Houses. Even before multiculturalism became a concept to be studied and promoted, it was a matter-of-fact reality in the building where my grandparents lived—a square, solid structure with a fairytale address: Sunny House on Mereweather Road. Built by the Nawab of Surat in 1897, the vast apartments of Sunny House were soon snapped up by Bombay's burgeoning middle class. The ground floor was occupied by The Crown and Anchor, an Irani restaurant that, as its name suggests, wooed the sailors and workers of the thriving port next door.

When the port went, the Irani restaurant started stocking biscuits, toothpaste and chilled Coca Colas for the local residents. Through the 1940s and '50s, one of the partners, Keki Irani's voice floated up from 'The Crown and Anchor', calling for maska-pav and nodding at customers from a counter that bore the sign:

> Man to man is so unjust
> I do not know which man to trust
> I have trusted many to my sorrow
> So pay today and not tomorrow.

One floor above The Crown and Anchor lived Mrs Moses, a grand old Jewish lady. Next to her were three Parsi families squeezed into one apartment. On the second floor were my Bohra Muslim grandparents. And across from them, the First Family of Indian Football.

Neville D'Souza was the superstar who scored a hat trick against Australia in the 1956 Melbourne Olympics. His bother Derek later became the coach of the Indian football team. While their mother Aileen D'Souza sang for Hindi films—thrilling me to bits when she popped up for a nano-second in the Rishi Kapoor and Dimple Kapadia starrer, *Bobby*.

One apartment on the third floor was owned by the Taj—the large living room converted into a dormitory for waiters and the rooms used to house employees and their families. The other apartment was where the tall and imposing Mildred Grant started Scholar School in 1961.

The long verandas running along Mandlik Road were open to the sights and sounds of Colaba. To Maruti Bandu Shinde, the cobbler across the road, who gave his savings to my grandfather for safekeeping; and who sent us a cake from La Patisserie every year after his son got a job at the Taj. To the children of Candy House, with whom my mother and her siblings become 'shouting friends'. To the shops downstairs, for whom Mrs Kotwal lowered a basket whenever she needed bread or buns. And, of course, to Taj Mahal Hotel with its lovely dome and glamourous goings on.

There were, however, other denizens of Colaba who were not quite as endearing. The bylanes near the Taj, with their cheap lodgings, had always attracted sailors and emigres, touts and tricksters. But by the 1970s, racy had become seedy. Hippies and drug-dealers slumped, unwashed and dazed, under porticos. Handsome buildings crumbled as landlords and tenants engaged in prolonged battles. One day, the lights at The Crown and Anchor dimmed and the friendly eatery metamorphosed into a dance bar—famous enough to figure in waggish articles. 'Nice girls don't even know about this place,' wrote a regular patron of that seedy den. 'And nice boys spend a lot of time there.'

Suddenly, Sunny House—and Colaba—felt vulnerable and shabby. Like the crumbling, slightly menacing neighbourhood in Anita Desai's *Baumgartner's Bombay*—a novel about gentle Hugo Baumgartner, who had escaped Nazi Germany and gradually grown old in Colaba, only to encounter evil in the form of a drug-crazed German hippie.

It had become an unnerving place in which Charles Sobhraj, serial killer and psychopath, stalked his prey. Where he took to targeting hippies near Dipti Drink House on Ormiston Road, looking for passports to steal, accomplices to recruit and women to murder.

It was the Colaba of Blue Nile, featuring Heavenly Helen and Sherry-Eyed Sharon. 'Life is a cabaret old chum,' declared the advertisements in the eveningers. Many seemed to agree, if the eager queues were any indication.

This was also the Colaba of Slip Disc, the grungy disco that was the scene of Mumbai's favourite rock story. Jimmy Page and Robert Plant of Led Zeppelin were staying at the Taj in 1972. Finding the hotel's disco too straitlaced, they wandered along the seafront to Slip Disc on Arthur Bunder Road. The doorman stopped them, saying that hippies were not allowed, but a music lover named Yusuf Gandhi thought he recognized the duo and ushered them inside. While Page and Plant sipped a beer and watched a local group called Synthesis, whispers zipped through the nightclub. Finally, the manager plucked up his courage and requested them to perform. The duo agreed, and a Colaba legend was born. 'We stopped in Bombay and we ended up playing in an old dive there for a bottle of Scotch,' Plant recalled years later. 'It was superb. I was singing through a Fender cabinet (that) was the size of a 12' telly and Pagey was playing a guitar that must have had piano strings on it. And the people were so happy because they'd never witnessed anybody just passing through, taking the trouble to stop and play.'

'Slip Disc was dark, heavy, boom boom in your chest,' recalls Sherree Carlos, who describes herself as a borderline member of that crowd and was in Slip Disc on the big night in 1972. 'I always laugh about how many guys I propped up as they threw up on the wall.'

Slip Disc was also where Atomic Forest performed—if the musicians were not too stoned to go through the motions. The psychedelic rock group was headed by Keith Kanga—notorious for his false teeth, his smoky-fuzzy sound, his ferocious Jehovah's Witness granny and his drug habit—who lived in the same building as my friend Farah. 'The band would jam and hang out at Jony Castle, a crumbling mansion in South Mumbai, where Kanga lived with his grandmother,' *Rolling Stone India* recalled in a feature some years ago. 'The mansion also housed a brothel and soon turned into a den of nefarious activities in true rock & roll tradition. Kanga and the rest of the band began experimenting with mind-altering substances.'

The musicians often spilled onto the pavement outside

Jony Castle with glazed eyes and unwashed hair. I dreaded these encounters, just as I dreaded running into the dreadlocked hippies and drug dealers who mysteriously materialized out of the night. They gave form and substance to the tales of drug smuggling and tragic addictions that inhabited the shadowy arcades and too-wild parties. The Colaba that I hurried through with averted eyes was the same locality that man-about-town Jamal Mecklai described in the Indian Heritage Society booklet: 'You want to buy some shoes? Or magazines? Or smuggled anything? And, of course, local wares?...try on some chappals, send some flowers to somebody, and, omigod, a venereal display of Studd release delay chewing gum for marital joy. Like I said, you can find anything on Causeway.'

What astounds me is that the Colaba of my grandmother and mother coexisted so matter-of-factly with Studd chewing gum. In their genteel dimension, J.J. Rodriguez conducted his 'Cours de Dance' classes and taught the rumba, the cha cha cha and the waltz to a motley crew of secretaries, managers and students. Jimmy sat at the counter of Paradise Restaurant and dispensed Scotch Broth, Chicken Lollies and 'Kem chhe kaleja?' to regulars. The two silver-haired ladies in Dit Randezvous d'Art adorned their shop window with embroidered doilies and dainty pillow covers.

'Antiques at Zal Contractors, bedsheets of yesteryears at Meena Bazaar, freshly ground coffee at Philips, a leather whip or two (if that's your fancy) at the roadside stalls, a gaping manhole, garab achaar at Swabals', Margaret Wong Shroff's garlic sauce at Tham's, a cracked rib if you fall onto a giant waterpipe, iced watermelon juice at Edward VIII's or soaking feet from a burst sewer down Causeway,' wrote Pearl Padamsee in an article in *The Evening News*, about the Causeway of the '70s and '80s, with its vast textile emporia and clothes shops. Not to forget the shoe shops 'where Dawood or Bashirbhai yell "Ek saw tera number, size five" to shorter versions of themselves hiding in the mezzanine, after which the boxes land miraculously at your feet.' 'There are other people, places, things, we know, but ask the regulars. Those cosmopolitan connoisseurs—let's say the Mirandas, Jaffreys, Watsas, Saldanhas, Kotwals, Gursahanis, Moraes, Patels, and Padamsees,' she concludes. 'They'll shop and risk a manhole: Colaba is still their scene.'

It is still my scene too. Many old acquaintances have gone—Swabal and Aga Bros; Paradise and Edward VIII; Modern Stores and Variety Stores; Purple Pussycat and even Crown and Anchor. And as Chitra Lalwani says, 'The whole strip has changed.' But new friends have come along—Theobroma and Café Churchill and vendors who vend Grinch pyjamas and Zara tops for 300 bucks.

Colaba is the only place I know where the toy shop, Souvenirs, does a monsoon display of Barbies in hijab for the plane-loads of Arabs who descend every year. And where the all-purpose Bhavya Stores once hailed Independence Day with a creative window display of orange, green and white underwear. Where men from Bihar lure you with their irresistible patter: 'Zara, Mango. Partywear, tops, jumpsuit, long dresses. Dekh lo. Dekh lo.' Where shops like Rajsi Bros supply traditional textiles and scarves called kangas to large expanses of Africa. And display posters with ominous messages in the ilk of:

> Love your job
> But never love your company
> Because you never know when your company will stop loving you.

Forget about the Grinch pyjamas. Where else will you encounter such random nuggets of wisdom?

If it's business as usual on the Causeway, it's better business than usual in the bylanes. Here, grunge is giving way to gentrification. Sunny House, for example, has a famous artist living on the top floor, a swish art gallery on the first floor, and a shop selling vintage trunks and luggage on the ground floor. The buildings next door boast cool eateries and cafes.

Down the road are boutiques that specialize in kitsch, antiques and exquisite clothes. Artists and galleries have discovered the lofty ceilings and charm of Mandlik Road, Arthur Bunder Road, Wodehouse Road. The media informs us that Colaba is now the Art District of Mumbai.

But then Colaba has always been open to the wind and the waves and new ideas. With that has come poetry, music, quirks and, sometimes, danger. It was these very waves and winds that brought the terrorists into Mumbai in 2008. The men who strode through the neighbourhood, smashing dreams, glass window panes and the casual trust of centuries.

My uncle in Sunny House heard the rat-a-tat of a machine gun, followed by a loud Bmmmfff. He rushed to his window and saw surreal sights. Hands sticking out from the grill near the hotel swimming pool, waving and waving. Asking for help. Blood-soaked guests stumbling out from the back door. Flames licking the familiar, friendly dome.

The next evening, I took my three tiny daughters to the terrace of our building. Smoke from the Taj and the Oberoi smudged the sky with grey. Ugly sounds came from the direction of Nariman House where, for the last five years, a Jewish centre and synagogue was being run. Helicopters circled my world, hovering above the Fort Convent and Wodehouse Cathedral; Sargent House and Colaba Bazaar. I remember the overwhelming sense of loss. How could things ever be the same? How could Colaba ever return to its easy, adaptable self?

Incredibly, the Taj reopened after two short years.

Colaba took longer to open the doors that it slammed shut on that blood-and-smoke-filled night. But slowly, my patch of hornblende, feldspar and once-sea is again allowing optimism and belief to blow in with the sea breeze.

Once again Colaba stands, amidst a soupy sea, open to the winds and waves; to migratory dragonflies and blue kingfishers; to differences and to brave ideas.

Joe Ravi

The Taj Mahal Hotel as it stands today. *Source: Wikimedia Commons.* (*CC-BY-SA 3.0*)

10. Seeking the Past

MY STORY IS ALMOST DONE. ALL THAT'S LEFT IS A CLUE HUNT to complete and fragments of the past to find. I examine my list:

- A stone in the compound of the Colaba Police Station, which marks the departure point for the ferry from Old Woman's Island to Bombay.
- A tree that once grew at Colaba Station.
- The original railings of the station.
- A mango tree that fruited twice a year, and stood in the garden of Mrs Hough, daughter of the land-grabbing General Waddington, who appeared so early in this tale.
- The gate of a fisherman's wharf that has now been incorporated into a temple near Arthur Bunder.

I start my quest at the Colaba Police Station. I've managed to find a rare picture of the stone that marks the landing place of that long-ago ferry between Old Woman's Island and Bombay. I know exactly what I'm seeking. This time, I march through the police compound and head straight to the gate of the Kshirsagar abode. Ignoring the young man in the courtyard, I peep shamelessly and spot the stone. It's been painted light blue and cloaked in a dirty, brown rag.

'That's no way to treat a monument,' I think.

'How can a family be allowed to build a house in the middle of the police station compound and fence off a city landmark?' I think next.

'But then what does the stone tell us anyway?' I wonder finally. I know nothing now that I didn't before. I can imagine nothing now that I couldn't before.

Even so, I head to Badhwar Park, past the iron railings that may or may not have a history. The glorious baobab tree is exactly where Mr Aklekar had told me it would be. Not only does it stand on the front lawn, it also has a helpful sign that announces: 'Adesonia Digitata. This tree occupied a vantage point of the old Colaba Railway Station. Tree remains even after station is gone. Trees are forever.'

The baobabs are supposed to have travelled to India along with the Portuguese and many are 400 years old. Which makes it very likely that this tree witnessed the arrival of the British, the polite world of Mrs Hough, the bustle of the cotton trade, and now the catch-catch-playing children of Badhwar Park.

Perhaps the baobab tree knows where the overachieving mango tree stands, but nobody else does. So I head to Radio Club to hunt for the old gate instead.

Saurab Rao

This glorious Baobab tree is all that remains of the old Colaba Station.

I soon realize that looking for temples in Colaba Bazaar is a bit like looking for shiny slippers on the Causeway. I'm spoilt for choice. I'm taking a deep breath and wondering which temple to start with, when the foolishness of my quest strikes me.

The past doesn't live in railings and gates. Or even in lovely baobab and mango trees. It lives in the easy cosmopolitanism, and the ability to 'thoda sa adjust kar lo'.

It lives in the Midnight Mass at Afghan Church, where

all manner of Colabawalas—members of the congregation, officers from the cantonment, scientists from TIFR, people who love Christmas carols and heritage churches—gather beneath the dark wood rafters on Christmas Eve.

It lives in the aroma of Bottle Masala and Dhansaak powder; hing and attar; marijuana and urine that infuse the bombil-tinged air. It lives in 100-year-old buildings with their friendly ghosts. And in poets and pianists, footballers and wall-jumpers, schoolgirls in beige sacks and the beady-eyed creators of those beige sacks, who together continue to write the unique history of Colaba.

Acknowledgements

IN SOME WAYS, THIS IS THE MOST DAUNTING SECTION TO tackle. After all this book is the sum of the stories, anecdotes and recollections of so many people. Grand-aunts and neighbours, local historians and old-timers. To everybody who has brought life and colour to my Colaba, thank you.

An especially resounding thank you to Deepak Rao—Mumbai's most dedicated archivist—who shared his wealth of history, memories and newspaper clippings.

Thank you to Priya Pathiyan, Sherree Carlos, Ziya Maskati, Sakib Maskati, Ganesh Nakhawa, Munis Varawalla, Jimmy Baria, Chiku Advani and Rajendra Aklekar for all the fascinating conversations and inputs.

Thank you also to Naresh Fernandes and Jerry Pinto for ideas, suggestions and conversations about defunct dance bars and long-forgotten piano teachers.

And, of course, a big thank you to my editor Radhika Shenoy, who came up with the idea of this book in the first place, and stayed patient and cheerful even when I wobbled.

Bibliography

Anderson, Philip. *The English in western India*. Smith, Taylor & Co., 2019.

Anonymous, James M. Campbell, Reginald Edward Enthoven. *Gazetteer of the Bombay Presidency*. British Library, 2011.

Aubrey, D. *Letters from Bombay*. Remington & CO., 1884.

Bromfield, Louis. *Night in Bombay*. Harper & Brothers Publishers, 1940.

Burnell, John. *Bombay in the Days of Queen Anne—Being an Account of the Settlement Also: Burnell's Narrative of His Adventures in Bengal.* Read Books, 2007.

Caine, William Sproston. *Picturesque India: A Handbook for European Travellers*. G. Routledge, 1891.

Coleman, Bill. *Trumpet Story*. Palgrave Macmillan, 1989.

Cunha, J. Gerson Da. *The Origin of Bombay*. Forgotten Books, 2018.

Dalvi, Mustansir. '"This New Architecture": Contemporary Voices on Bombay's Architecture Before the Nation State.' *Tekton: A Journal of Architecture, Urban Design and Planning,* Vol 5, Issue 1 (March 2018): pp. 56–73

Dantwala, M.L. *A Hundred Years of Indian Cotton.* The East India Cotton Association Ltd, 1947.

Davidar, David. *The Solitude of Emperors.* Aleph Book Company, 2013.

Desai, Anita. *Baumgartner's Bombay: A Novel.* Mariner Books 2000

Douglas, James J.P. *Glimpses of Old Bombay and Western India: With Other Papers.* Sampson Low, Marston and Company, 1900

Dwivedi, Sharda and Rahul Mehrotra. *Fort Walks: Around Bombay's Fort Area.* Eminence Designs, 1999.

Edwardes, Stephen Meredyth. *The Bombay City Police: A Historical Sketch, 1672-1916.* H. Milford, Oxford University Press, 1923

_____*By-ways of Bombay.* D.B. Taraporevala Sons & Co., 1912.

_____*The Rise of Bombay: A Retrospect.* Times of India Press, 1902.

Fernandes, Naresh. *Taj Mahal Foxtrot: The Story of Bombay's Jazz Age.* Lustre/Roli Books, 2012

Forrest, Edmund William. *Ned Fortescue,* or *Roughing It*

Through Life: A Story Founded on Fact. Forgotten Books, 2018.

Govind Narayan's Mumbai: An Urban Biography from 1863. Translated by Murali Ranganathan. Anthem Press, 2009.

Harker, Lizzie Allen. *Jan and Her Job.* Charles Scribner's Sons, 1917.

Hobbs, Major H. *John Barleycorn Bahadur: Old Time Taverns in India.* Thacker, Spink & Co, 1944.

Kanga, Firdaus. *Trying to Grow*. Ravi Dayal Publishers, 1990.

Kunte, B.G., ed. *Mahatma Gandhi in Maharashtra (1915 to 1946)*. Vol 9, *Source Material for a History of the Freedom Movement in India*. Government of India, 1980.

Lala, R.M. *For the Love of India: The Life and Times of Jamsetji Tata.* Portfolio, 2006.

——*The Creation of Wealth: The Tatas from the 19th to the 21st Century*. Penguin Books India, 2006.

Maclean, James MacKenzie. *Guide to Bombay: Historical, Statistical, and Descriptive*. Bombay Gazette Steam Press, 1889.

Marfatia, Meher. 'Whose Lane Is It Anyway?' *Midday*, 2016.

Mehta, Vinod. *Lucknow Boy*. Penguin, 2011.

Moses, Henry. *Sketches of India: With Notes on the Seasons, Scenery and Society of Bombay, Elephanta, and Salsette.* London, Simpkin, Marshall & Co., 1750.

Naidu, Leela with Jerry Pinto. *Leela: A Patchwork Life*. Penguin Books India, 2012.

Nixseaman, A.J. *The Afghan War Memorial Church, and Historical Notes on Colaba*. Thacker, 1938.

Ovington, John. *A Voyage to Surat in the Year 1689*. Oxford Humphrey Milford/Oxford University Press, 1929.

Padamsee, Alyque. *A Double Life: My Exciting Years in Theatres and Advertising*. Penguin, 2000.

Peterson, Margaret. *Just Because*. Palala Press, 2016.

Philip, Anderson. *The English in Western India*. Bibliolife, 2009.

Pinder, D.A. *Visitor's Illustrated Guide to Bombay*. G. Claridge & Co.1904.

Pinto, Jerry and Naresh Fernandes. *Bombay, Meri Jaan: Writings on Mumbai*. Penguin India, 2003.

Pinto, Sarah Ann. *Lunatic Asylums in Colonial Bombay: Shackled Bodies, Unchained Minds*. Palgrave Macmillan, 2018.

Ranade, Rekha. *Sir Bartle Frere and His Times: A Study of His Bombay Years, 1862-1867*. Mittal Publications, 1990.

Rau, Santha Rama. *Home to India*. Victor Gollancz, 1946.

Riding, Tim. '"Making Bombay Island": Land Reclamation and Geographical Conceptions of Bombay, 1661-1728.' *Journal of Historical Geography* 59 (January 2018): 27-39.

Roth, Cecil. *The Sassoon Dynasty*. Robert Hale Limited, London 1941.

Rushdie, Salman. *Midnight's Children*. Vintage, 2012.

_____*The Moor's Last Sigh*. Vintage, 2006.

Scott, Clement. *The Wheel of Life: A Few Memories and Recollections*. Wentworth Press, 2019.

Sharpe, W.R.S. *The Port of Bombay*. Bombay Port Trust, 1930.

Sheppard, Samuel T. *Bombay*. Times of India Press. 1932.

_____1880. *Bombay Place-names and Street-names: An Excursion into the By-ways of the History of Bombay City*. Franklin Classics, 2018.

The BC and CI Railway Magazine, 1943.

The Examiner, 1905.

Times of India Directories of the 1920s and 1930s.

Twain, Mark. *Following the Equator: A Journey around the World*. The American Publishing Company, 1897.

Wren, Percival Christopher. *Soldiers of Misfortune*. Frederick A. Stokes Company, 1929.

Zubrzycki, John. *The Mysterious Mr Jacob: Diamond Merchant, Magician and Spy*. Penguin Books India, 2012.

ALSO IN SPEAKING TIGER

Shivaji Park

Dadar 28: History, Places, People

Shanta Gokhale

One of the earliest planned neighbourhoods of Bombay, Shivaji Park in Dadar was conceived in order to decongest the mega city's residential and commercial centre after the plague epidemic of 1896. With its massive playground named after the Maratha warrior king, gorgeous Art Deco buildings and the great Arabian Sea beyond, Shivaji Park was a coveted residential area long before Bandra and Juhu.

In this little gem of a biography, Shanta Gokhale, author, cultural critic and longtime resident of the area, brings together key events and individuals to create a matchless portrait of the neighbourhood. Through her conversations with friends and neighbours, she relives the thrill and novelty of moving from congested chawls to flats that ensured privacy and the unheard-of luxury of piped gas back in the 1930s. She recalls the politically charged decades of the 1950s and '60s, when P.K. Atre's voice reverberated through the grounds of Shivaji Park during the United Maharashtra Movement and Bal Thackeray launched the Shiv Sena. She also writes of the illustrious people who have contributed to the cultural fabric of Shivaji Park: the freedom fighter Senapati Bapat; town planner N.V. Modak; classical musician Sharadchandra Arolkar; veteran actress Sulabha Deshpande; and cricketers Sachin Tendulkar and Vinod Kambli, among others. The designated playground of the neighbourhood, she argues, is also one of the city's most democratic spaces where hundreds walk every morning and evening in the shade of tall and gracious trees; where people young and old gather around the 'katta' to talk politics or share a moment of love. And even as she celebrates the grace and spirit of Shivaji Park, Gokhale also notes how, despite the best efforts of its residents, the area is threatened by rampant redevelopment, and how the sense of community that has always defined it is slowly eroding.

Page Extent: 184 pp | Price: ₹499

ALSO IN SPEAKING TIGER

Chandni Chowk

The Mughal City of Old Delhi

Swapna Liddle

'A wonderful and much-needed introduction to the history of the Old City of Delhi and a welcome addition to the literature on Shahjahanabad.'—William Dalrymple

What we know today as Chandni Chowk was once a part of one of the greatest cities of the world—the imperial city established by the Mughal emperor Shahjahan in the seventeenth century, and named after him—Shahjahanabad. This is the story of how the city came to be established, its grandeur as the capital of an empire at its peak, and its important role in shaping the language and culture of North India. It is also the story of the many tribulations the city has seen—the invasion of Nadir Shah, the Revolt of 1857, Partition.

Today, Shahjahanabad has been subsumed under the gigantic sprawl of metropolitan Delhi. Yet it has an identity that is distinct. Popularly known as Chandni Chowk, its name conjures up romantic narrow streets, a variety of street food and exotic markets. For Shahjahanabad is still very much a living city, though the lives of the people inhabiting it have changed over the centuries. Dariba Kalan still has rows of flourishing jewellers' shops; Begum Samru's haveli is now Bhagirath Palace, a sprawling electronics market, and no visit to Chandni Chowk is complete without a meal at Karim's, whose chefs use recipes handed down to them through the ages for their mouth-watering biriyani and kebabs.

Swapna Liddle draws upon a wide variety of sources, such as the accounts of Mughal court chroniclers, travellers' memoirs, poetry, newspapers and government documents, to paint a vivid and dynamic panorama of the city from its inception to recent times.

Page Extent: 196 pp | Price: ₹499

ALSO IN SPEAKING TIGER

Connaught Place

and the Making of New Delhi

Swapna Liddle

'The value of this book is that it interweaves the familiar story of how New Delhi was built, with social history and reflections on the future of the capital city. An excellent introduction for both inhabitants and visitors.'—Narayani Gupta, Historian

The origin of New Delhi can be traced to the Coronation Durbar in December 1911, where Emperor George V announced the transfer of the capital of the British Empire in India from Calcutta to Delhi.

Swapna Liddle traces in fascinating detail the events that led up to that historic day: the deliberations over the choice of location; the roles played by the Viceroy, Lord Hardinge, and the two principal architects, Edwin Lutyens and Herbert Baker; and, finally, the naming of the capital as 'New Delhi'—to distinguish it from the old city of Shahjahanabad.

Even as the new capital took shape, it was Connaught Place that gave life to the city. Designed as a shopping and commercial centre for the elite—both British and Indian—it boasted of the most exclusive shops, cinemas and restaurants.

While many of the old familiar haunts like Gaylord, Volga and Regal Cinema have shut their doors, Connaught Place continues to reinvent itself with shiny new multiplexes, branded stores and restaurants taking their place. A guidebook of the early 1940s described Connaught Place as 'indeed the most fashionable shopping centre…and, undoubtedly the most progressive part of the most progressive town in the country.' The crowds that continue to throng its corridors, both young and old, visitors to the city and residents alike, bear testimony to the statement.

Page Extent: 196 pp | Price: ₹499

ALSO IN SPEAKING TIGER

Thamel

Dark Star of Kathmandu

Rabi Thapa

'A moody, elegant portrait of an emblematic neighbourhood as it has changed through time... This is a richly storied book, and one that captures the energy and verve of contemporary Kathmandu.'—Manjushree Thapa

For long a sleepy rural enclave, Thamel is today the beating commercial and cultural heart of Kathmandu—a dizzying square kilometre of hotels, bars, cafés, bookshops and temples to which visitors and residents gravitate, drawn by its dazzle and its possibilities.

In this unusual biography of the place, Rabi Thapa revisits the haunts of his youth. Tramping around its temples and monasteries, he unravels its layered history as well as the tales of the kings, monks and travelling merchants who laid its foundations. From residents—both Nepali and those who visited and never left—he pieces together the story of Kathmandu of the 'flower-power' sixties, the legendary Freak Street, and the rise of modern Thamel. On its streets he encounters glue-sniffing children, local toughs battling for turf, transvestite prostitutes turning tricks, and entrepreneurs looking to make it big. What emerges is a finely detailed portrait of a place that is not only a vibrant, ever-evolving reflection of the social mores of Kathmandu, but also an enduring staging post for Western fantasies of the East.

Written in the best traditions of flânerie, *Thamel* combines history, memoir and sharp reportage to tell the electric story of a place forever in flux, forever reinventing itself to suit the appetites and desires of those who seek it out.

Page Extent: 184 pp | Price: ₹399